EDUCATING TEACHERS: CRITIQUES AND PROPOSALS

Douglas Myers & Fran Reid, editors

Symposium Series/4
The Ontario Institute for Studies in Education

The opinions stated in this publication are those of the contributors and, as such, do not necessarily represent the point of view of the Institute.

The Ontario Institute for Studies in Education has three
prime functions: to conduct programs of graduate study in education,
to undertake research in education, and to assist in
the implementation of the findings of educational studies.
The Institute is a college chartered by an Act of the Ontario
Legislature in 1965. It is affiliated with the University of
Toronto for graduate studies purposes.

© The Ontario Institute for Studies in Education 1974
252 Bloor Street West, Toronto, Ontario M5S 1V6

ISBN 0-7744-0100-1   Printed in Canada

Contents

	Introduction/*Douglas Myers and Fran Reid*	1
Part One	**The Context and Objectives of Teacher Education**	
	Some Prior Questions/*Brian S. Crittenden*	9
	Radical Notes/*John McMurtry*	27
	How Not to Reform a Teacher Education System: Ontario 1966–1971/*Douglas Myers and David Saul*	33
	Avoiding Guaranteed Failure/*Verner Smitheram and Eric S. Hillis*	52
	Continuing Education: A Neglected Concept/ *Robert Gidney, Philip Linden, and Geoffrey Milburn*	69
Part Two	**Some Innovative Programs**	
	Teacher Education: *Soufflé de fromage*, or Cheese Omelet?/*Myer Horowitz*	81
	A Concurrent Program in Scotland/*J. H. Duthie*	93
	The Implications of In-Service Programs/ *Donald Longwell*	98
	Teachers and Alternative Schools/*Robert Beardsley*	106
	A Role for the Research Scientist/*Robert Logan*	111
Part Three	**Future Directions**	
	Salvaging the Wreckage: Ontario 1971–1973/ *Douglas Myers*	117
	Research and Innovation in Teacher Education/ *J. H. Duthie*	127
	Teachers and Teaching Competencies/*John A. Tickle*	133
	A Diploma of Further Studies in Education/ *V. S. Ready*	141
	Bridging the Gap: Improving Cooperation between Teacher Educators and Teachers/ *George S. Tomkins*	145

Acknowledgments
The editors wish to express their appreciation to the staff of the Editorial Division of the Ontario Institute for Studies in Education for their patient encouragement. In particular, we thank Ruth Sims and Christine Purden for their expert assistance and advice.

Introduction

Douglas Myers and Fran Reid

As many contemporary critics of education have pointed out, schools have become an integral part of the assembly-line production model that characterizes industrial societies. This model fosters rigid interpretations of such concepts as "progress" and "growth" in economic and quantitative terms rather than in humanistic and qualitative ones. The effect is to obscure the fact that terms such as these refer to normative values that must be subjected to constant, careful scrutiny.

Schools, of course, have always been closely connected with their surrounding society, and they reflect and support prevailing social emphases to a greater or lesser degree. The question that we must examine is whether our public educational institutions have become primarily instruments for mass "schooling" instead of instruments for mass "education." The distinction between these terms is crucial: the first presupposes that certain concepts and values are truths and promotes them; the second encourages a constant scrutiny and evaluation of the premises on which our concepts and values are based.

In recent years, many have argued that the ideal of education increasingly has been subverted and that schooling has become the main purpose of our educational institutions. Everett Reimer, for example, has pointed out that schools combine four distinct social functions: custodial care, indoctrination, social role selection, and education (the last usually defined narrowly in terms of imparting skills and techniques geared toward modern industrial, corporate development). Mass schooling promotes the social mythology that students proceed through the system according to their innate individual ability. It ignores or de-emphasizes the factors that determine and define individual abilities and the ends to which they are put. The school slots into which the students fit are later reflected in the jobs, pay differentials, and corresponding power and privileges that the graduates achieve. Of course, the mass schooling system does not work perfectly. In fact it cannot, in a society that employs a rhetoric of equality yet is organized on an elite basis, that demands unlimited economic growth to solve its social and political difficulties yet is unable to cope with the inevitable result — pollution, urban chaos, growing alienation. The schools inevitably reflect such contradictions.

As a result, schools are under attack from both sides: from those who believe they do not perform their instrumental role of mass schooling with sufficient thoroughness, thrift, and efficiency; and from those who are disenchanted by mass education as an effective means of social reform. The present outcry against an education system that promised so much to so many is understandable. Though there is not yet wholesale support for entirely dismantling our system of public education, philosophical and ideological objections to it have found a powerful voice in the writings of Illich and others, governments are responding to taxpayers' complaints by cutting back on funds, and an increasing number of students are rejecting the schooling game by simply walking out.

Is it possible to redress the imbalance between schooling and education in our schools? Can we develop educational institutions that shift the primary emphasis from fitting people into narrow, inhibiting niches to enabling them to intervene directly in their own lives? The problem, as Paulo Freire puts it, is not so much lack of knowledge as it is a false perception of reality. The task is to reexamine and assess some of the basic concepts and values of our society so that we can reshape them in the light of present realities. The challenge is to live humanely in a highly technological society.

The schools cannot effect such a transformation independently. They can make an important contribution to the process, however, by providing an educational setting that encourages critical inquiry and analysis, and imaginative and independent judgment. In this, the role of the teacher is crucial. But because teachers are themselves the product of the present educational system they must first come to grips with their own schooling, sift their own perceptions of reality, and develop a critical awareness toward the values of their society. The institutions that educate prospective teachers should be committed to supporting them in this difficult task; too often they are not.

Teacher education is commonly referred to as teacher *training*, a term that underlines the concept of the teacher's function as an agent for schooling. Few would deny that there are important techniques and skills that must be mastered by those who wish to teach; but unless there is a primary emphasis on the ends that such means are intended to serve, and a searching exploration of the connections between the schools and the society that surrounds them, these techniques and skills exist in a vacuum. Such an emphasis is generally lacking in teacher education, and the result is that teachers most often see themselves as merely the implementers of educational policies conceived and directed by others. Not surprisingly, this situation produces widespread disillusionment and cynicism among teachers, and encourages and rewards the development of administrators with a narrow career orientation.

Perhaps because of the failure of teacher education institutions to address themselves to the fundamental philosophical, social, economic, and political issues involved in mass public education or to adequately prepare teachers to understand or cope with the realities of the system, few teachers regard their experience in a faculty of education or teachers' college with much nostalgia or respect. Indeed, there is perhaps no other occupation that holds its own preparation system in such contempt. Until teacher education institutions and, indeed, teachers themselves determine to educate and support teachers who will neither mystify nor be mystified, this will not change. The development and promotion of such an objective by teachers and their organizations would be an example of professional responsibility, in the best sense of that much-abused term.

This, then, is the context in which we hope this book will be read. Much has been written in global and far-reaching terms about the manifest defects of our education systems and the need for profound and radical improvement. Nonetheless, the question remains of where and how to start. We believe teacher education to be a crucially important area. The articles contained here by no means cover all the promising possibilities for development, nor can the suggestions they offer be taken as panaceas for the problems in this field. Rather, they examine some of the fundamental issues in teacher education and propose some of the first steps that must be taken if we are to move toward the profound and basic changes so badly needed.

In the first section, "The Context and Objectives of Teacher Education," the contributors address a number of these basic issues. Although they take very different positions on the question, both Brian Crittenden and John McMurtry examine some of the philosophical premises and purposes underlying teacher education. Using Ontario as a case study, Myers and Saul take a hard look at the political and institutional factors that have led up to recent changes in Ontario's teacher education system and consider whether these changes will really meet the need for reform. Moving on from this to a consideration of the relationship between faculties of education and universities, Smitheram and Hillis assess the relative merits and defects of concurrent and consecutive teacher education programs. Concluding this section, Gidney, Linden, and Milburn turn to an examination of the need for renewing the professional skills of teachers who are already qualified.

The emphasis in the second section is on recent innovative programs that have given rise to ideas for teacher education and might be worth applying more broadly. Myer Horowitz relates, in direct and personal terms, the advantages and disadvantages of the internship approach tried out at McGill University, and puts forward some principles concerning the field-experience component of teacher education. J. H. Duthie describes the combined undergraduate arts, science, and education program being tried out at the newly established Stirling University in Scotland and examines its implications. Donald Longwell draws on his experience with in-service teachers' courses for some ideas that he believes might also fruitfully be applied to pre-service teacher preparation. An experimental program for high school students recently introduced in Toronto has led two other contributors, Robert Beardsley and Robert Logan, to consider some new roles for teachers. Beardsley takes a thoughtful look at the question of how teachers can best be trained for work in alternative schools and makes some concrete suggestions as to the form that an "alternative school option" in teacher education programs might take. Logan, on the other hand, makes a case for involving research scientists in high school programs, a scheme that he feels would benefit students and teachers alike.

The contributors to the final section look to the years ahead, identifying areas where teacher education is still in urgent need of reform and examining some ways it might be brought about. Myers begins by surveying the present situation in Ontario and exploring the actions needed at both governmental and institutional levels if future programs for teachers are to be relevant and flexible enough to meet society's needs. Pursuing Myers's theme, Jack Duthie posits a framework for the reform of teacher education that would allow for the development and evaluation of new teacher education techniques prior to their implementation. Turning to more specific issues, John Tickle deals with how programs for teachers — especially at the elementary level — can be modified to improve their skills in the art of teaching. Vernon Ready, on the other hand, deals with the need for continuing education, offering, as one solution, the introduction of a widely recognized diploma for further studies in education. Finally, George Tomkins considers how the initial training and ongoing preparation of teachers can be wedded through a focus on curriculum development.

The insights into the nature and quality of teacher education that the contributors to this book offer are as varied as their backgrounds in the educational field. Some speak as administrators, others as academic theorists, still others as practicing educators actively involved in the classroom. But underlying the variety of perspectives is a common theme — what must be done to ensure that our teachers are highly skilled professionals, equipped to meet the challenges of a society in transition.

There is clearly no magic solution to the problems of teacher education, no single "right" way to prepare prospective teachers to cope with and participate in the life of their schools and their communities effectively and wisely. Like everyone else, teachers must ultimately educate themselves. But teacher education institutions provide a structure and setting that either encourages and enhances or delays and inhibits that process. Upon teachers depends the degree to which our schools are able to "educate" as well as "school" our children. Upon teacher education institutions, therefore, rests a heavy and twofold responsibility. Initially, they must try to provide prospective teachers with access to the techniques and competencies of teaching, with a spirit of active, critical involvement in educational issues, and with a sense of community and of social context. At the same time, these institutions must take new initiatives to tap the great potential of experienced teachers in the field, drawing upon their talents not only to improve pre-service teacher education, but also to develop policies and programs that will assist practicing teachers in their own continuing professional and personal development. This is a daunting task, certainly, but beyond doubt it is also the most important single enterprise toward the reform of contemporary education.

PART ONE

The Context and Objectives of Teacher Education

Some Prior Questions

Brian S. Crittenden

The question of how teachers should be educated cannot be answered in any detail unless one takes a position, at least implicitly, on several other crucial questions.[1] Two are of particular importance. First, how much of the existing institutional form and social context of education is to be taken as given? Second, how is the process of education to be interpreted? After I have examined these questions, some basic issues in the conduct of teacher education can be more effectively explored.

The Social Context of Education
However we interpret the nature of education, the school is inevitably part of a complex pattern of interacting social and political institutions. The decisions we reach about the appropriate training of teachers will depend in part on how much of this arrangement we are prepared to take for granted. May we, or should we, accept as given the present institutional form of elementary and secondary schooling in our society? If so, we can decide what training teachers need by examining the kinds of tasks they are expected to perform in this system. Or should we consider reforming the system itself? In this case, to adjust teacher training to things as they are in the schools would at best ensure greater efficiency in doing what is undesirable.

If we agree that the criteria of teacher education should not simply reflect the present practice of schooling, should we at least accept as given the various social, economic, and political policies on the role of the school and concentrate on devising a form of teacher education that will improve the *educational* quality of what the schools do? Perhaps so; at least, this may be necessary in practice. But some of these policies clearly affect the character of the educational process itself. If they were changed, there would be significant consequences for teacher education. Suppose, for example, that the present law on compulsory schooling were revised so that attendance became optional after, say, fourteen years of age, and that the significance of the school as an instrument of economic selection and advancement were substantially diminished. The secondary school population would drop appreciably, there would be a sharp rise in the proportion of those who attended school because they were interested in the activities of formal education, and the school would relinquish much of its onerous and educationally distracting task as a sorting agency for industry and the university. Teachers in the high school would not need to spend nearly as much time performing the tasks of attendants in a day-care center and offering all kinds of "learning experiences" as alternatives to the serious work of education.

The sort of change I have just been considering obviously could not be effected without a radical reorganization of the economic life of society. Various options would have to be made available for those who chose to leave school at the age of fourteen. Perhaps the most important of these would be a new system of apprenticeships for practically every kind of work. And this might be related to the provision of general education for adults, in both full-time and part-time programs. Paul Goodman and others have made a strong case against compulsory schooling and the predominantly instrumental role of the school in our economy.[2] I believe, therefore, that such social and other policies, which so directly affect the practice of education, should *not* be accepted as part of the settled context within which we plan the improvement of teacher education.

Of course, some people will argue that even this proposal does not go far enough; that our society can be adequately reformed only by the violent overthrow of the whole present order. Because they see the school as inextricably bound to the dominant values of the sociopolitical system, they reject any direct attempt to reform the schools (including teacher education) as futile, holding that the only defensible procedure for teachers and students is to politicize thoroughly the institution of the school, to use it in whatever way possible to foment the revolution. Far from attempting to repair the weaknesses of schooling within the present society, they advocate the exploitation of these weaknesses in order to provoke a total breakdown.

This view illustrates the general point we are discussing: that proposals for the reform of teacher education will reflect in some fashion a decision on the educational and other social arrangements that are accepted as establishing the boundaries of the problem. In my opinion, however, the advocacy of the extreme position is mistaken, because there is an adequate provision in the accepted fundamental values and procedures of our society for attacking and reforming its manifest defects. The possibilities of peaceful change are such that I believe no reasonable case can be made at the present time to justify the risk of greater evil through revolution.

Moreover, I would challenge the assumption that the institutions of education simply do, or must inevitably, reflect the attitudes and values that prevail in the political and economic arrangements of our society. Of course, the school is shaped by specific social, political, economic, and technological conditions, and it should be responsive to them. But to the extent that it is concerned with the criteria of knowledge and belief and with the justification of values, it can claim an autonomous role in relation to these conditions. It is answerable to standards that have human currency or at least reflect the achievements of a culture. These standards are not static, but at any given time they provide a relatively broad perspective from which the school can critically evaluate the prevailing practices and fashions of the society, and so make a specifically educational contribution to social reform. This freedom can be very easily stifled. But in our society there is at least an underlying tradition of respect for reasoned inquiry and, to use the term broadly, academic freedom. In the present context, the point I wish to make is that to some extent the schools can be agents of social change without either turning into a subversive military operation or closing down until the whole social order is overthrown by revolution.

I have already asserted that in reforming teacher education we should not take for granted the present social expectations and policies for the conduct of schooling; but a further problem remains. Suppose that it is conceded that changes at this level (for example, in the compulsory attendance law) are desirable, but are simply not feasible, or would take a long time to effect. Since there is an opportunity to alter the pattern of teacher education here and now, should we not proceed directly with this task regardless of the wider context? Might we not even be able to reform the practice of schooling by reforming teacher education? I think not. What I have tried to say is that when we come to the details of reform in teacher education we must take a stand one way or the other on the present social arrangements that affect the school.

There are some fairly obvious difficulties in planning public teacher education autonomously. In the first place, no group has the authority to act this way in a democracy. Neither the teaching profession nor any other body would be justified in devising a program of teacher education that systematically ignored conditions of schooling that were an expression of public policy or even of widespread popular opinion. Second, no matter what changes are made within teacher education itself, they cannot possibly solve the problems of primary and secondary education that arise directly from social, political, and economic practices. Comprehensive reform of education is not possible unless attention is given simultaneously to the school in its social context and to training teachers.

But even when the latter is being fashioned in order to satisfy what one takes to be undesirable conditions of schooling, it does not follow that nothing worthwhile can be done. Although at this point I begin to anticipate the second of the questions to be discussed, I think it can fairly be assumed that certain teaching skills and activities form part of schooling, regardless of the details of educational theory and institutional form. We can at least set out to reform or improve some specific features of teacher education without waiting for the grand scheme of reform that will usher in the utopian age.

The Process of Education
Any serious program for the professional training of teachers must reflect an interpretation of the nature of education. The second prior question, then, is what the process of education should be like in childhood and adolescence.[3] Logically, this question comes before the issue of form and social context. We cannot evaluate the fittingness of institutional and administrative arrangements unless we know something about the nature of the enterprise they are supposed to serve. The two questions are, however, closely related, and I will refer to both in commenting on some diverse interpretations of education and their consequences for the training of teachers.

In order to reduce the topic to manageable proportions, I will make the following assumptions:
1. In the broadest sense, *education* refers to the activities involved in an individual's growing to maturity as a human being in a certain social and cultural context.
2. Some deliberate effort on the part of the adult members of society is necessary if the new members are to acquire the skills for thinking, feeling, and acting in distinctively human ways. I am assuming, in other words, that such skills do not form part of our genetic endowment or emerge later in a purely spontaneous way. The deliberate effort required constitutes a somewhat narrower sense of *education*.
3. In a society and culture as complex as ours, it is desirable (if not necessary) for the deliberate process of educating to take on some kind of distinct and systematic form and for certain appropriately trained people to be assigned special responsibility for conducting a significant part of the process.

I realize that some people will consider that even these assumptions grant too much. If their views were correct, however, there would seem to be no place for teachers, at least of the kind who needed special skills, and thus no point in arguing about what their training should be like.

There are at least three ways of responding to the question of what education (and the role of the school) should be. Each has certain consequences for teacher education. While features of one interpretation may be included in another, it is the dominant emphasis that makes a significant difference in practice.

1. *Education as predominantly a process of socialization.* This theory takes a variety of forms. In the most obvious version, the crucial object of education is to equip human beings with the beliefs, attitudes, and skills they need in order to fill happily and usefully the main roles that life in their society requires of them. I leave aside the question of who decides in detail what the needs of society are and which of them the school should try to satisfy. In practice, the basic task of education (and the school) is thought to consist of providing whatever prevocational training will satisfy the society's professional, industrial, commercial, and military needs. The school is expected also to encourage a willing acceptance of the values that prevail in the present social, political, and economic order, and to promote a strong sense of national identity. Thus, if our economic system depends on a spirit of rugged competition, the school will encourage it from an early age; if another country is thought to be a threat to our national security, the school will provoke the appropriate attitudes of mistrust; if industry is short of scientists, the school will put more emphasis on the teaching of science; if automation enables people to have much more free time, the school will give attention to hobbies and other leisure activities.

In another version of this theory, the instrumental role of the school is interpreted much more broadly. One of its general principles seems to be that if instruction or study of some kind can help to alleviate any contemporary social problem — from driving an automobile safely to using sex safely — it should form part of education in the schools.

Yet another form of this theory envisages the school as the comprehensive socializing agency. It has responsibility for every aspect of the child's development. It replaces the educational role of the family and substitutes for the lack of a vital educational influence in the general life of the community. Where there is concern for equality of opportunity, the school is expected to break down class differences and offset social conditions that are obstacles to scholastic achievement (and thus to social and economic opportunity). The school is seen as a conglomerate of family, community center, mental health clinic, and social reform agency. The traditional belief that education (at least in the school) is the key to ameliorating all society's ills is one expression of this theory.

A combination of these interpretations of the socialization theory, in both its conservative and reformative aspects, enjoys wide professional and popular support at the present time. I think it is correct to say that the majority of people in our society value education mainly for the economic opportunity it gives them.

From the point of view of teacher education, the significance of the socialization theory in all its forms is that it requires the school to engage in an enormous variety of activities. The underlying principle almost comes to this: the school should perform any socially useful service for young people that is not being provided elsewhere in the society, either because no other suitable agency exists or because the institutions that traditionally provided it have failed. But if the practice of schooling under this theory is thought to be desirable (or, indeed, inevitable), the designers of teacher education must consider whether there should not be a clear division of labor in the training of staff for such a multifarious enterprise. They should also consider whether a university education is necessary or even desirable for the kind of teaching required. Certainly, this theory offers no good reason for associating teachers' colleges exclusively with universities.

A complicating factor is that many supporters of the socialization theory, particularly in the third form mentioned, are not suggesting simply that the school should be the center for other activities (for example, counseling and social work) besides teaching in the more or less traditional sense. They are advocating a reinterpretation of the concepts of education and teaching. They want to emphasize a shift from learning in a fairly academic sense to one in which the teacher plays a very broad pastoral role. He is to be an expert in promoting the general development of the child, concerned as much, if not more, with the child's mental health and the conditions of his social environment as with conceptual skills. He must therefore combine the roles of parent, psychiatrist, social worker, and reformer with whatever part of the more narrowly pedagogical role society expects him to take. Apart from challenging the basic value of this interpretation as an ideal, I think it creates some serious practical questions for teacher education. Given a reasonable standard of proficiency, how many years would such multiprofessional training require? Among people entering the teaching profession in this country, how many would have the ability and energy to undertake this program? Assuming that some students want to spend more of their school time in fairly systematic academic study, where and how will their teachers be trained?

2. *Education as growth through the satisfaction of felt needs and interests.* According to this theory, the child is depicted as innately good, unfolding to a state of fulfillment through natural stages determined by an inner principle of growth. The theory was given its first significant expression by Jean-Jacques Rousseau, developed in the mystical educational writings of Froebel and Pestalozzi, and incorporated with some modifications in Dewey's more complex account of education. It radically rejects the interpretation of the child as a piece of material to be molded and of learning as the transfer of a body of information from one mental receptacle to another. Its own characteristic metaphor is the child as a plant. Pestalozzi expressed the image in this way:

> Sound education stands before me symbolized by a tree planted near fertilizing water. A little seed, which contains the design of the tree, its forms and proportions, is placed in the soil. See how it germinates and expands into trunk, branches, leaves, flowers and fruit! The whole tree is an uninterrupted chain of organic parts, the plan of which existed in its seed and root. Man is similar to the tree. In the new born child are hidden those faculties which are to unfold during life.[4]

At least as the expression of an ideal, this style of thought enjoys considerable popularity at the present time. It is reflected, for example, in the statements of two recent public committees on education: the Plowden Report in England and the Hall–Dennis Report in Ontario.[5] It reflects the contemporary resurgence of romanticism and the "do-your-own-thing" doctrine. It also appeals strongly to those who are committed to a predominantly individualist concept of freedom. And it is a convenient theory for the supporters of democratic equality in education: everyone's interests are of equal educational relevance, and the interpretation of what counts as an educational activity is such that differences of ability have virtually no significance.

In the process of education, this view places special emphasis on the child's native curiosity and enthusiasm for learning (if it is not stifled by inept adults), his creative capacities, and his ability to discover knowledge for himself. The techniques of instructing and of evaluating the learner according to objective standards of achievement are treated as educationally suspect. Whether proponents of this theory emphasize natural stages of growth or the satisfaction of felt needs and interests, it is evident that the teacher's role is almost entirely a negative one. Above all, he is to be a warm and loving person ready to respond to the learner's request for assistance, perhaps occasionally intervening to remove an obstacle to the ongoing process of growth or self-realization. If one takes the theory seriously, it is difficult to see how a curriculum of any kind can be justified. Moreover, since the teacher must be ready to respond to each child's or adolescent's felt needs and interests, it is difficult to envisage what course of training could possibly be appropriate. Certainly, there is no reason to assume that the academic studies of a university would be relevant. Apart from ensuring that teachers have (or acquire) the right kind of personality traits, a teacher education program might make them familiar with the typical felt needs and interests of children and adolescents, especially if they are required to spend several hours each day in a place called "school" along with a group of adults called "teachers." In any case, one wonders why the exponents of this theory would think the society should have any school attendance at all.

My main purpose here is not to offer a critique of the theory; I would, however, make two observations. First, the view of the child and of education presented by the growth theorists is not the only alternative to the inhumane practice of rote memorization — usually carried out without any understanding — which utterly stifles initiative. And second, proponents of the theory usually introduce normative criteria for distinguishing "growth" from other kinds of change, and desirable felt needs and interests from those that are undesirable; thus, objective criteria are smuggled into the educational process, and adults take a hand, though surreptitiously, in shaping its direction.

3. *Education as initiation into public traditions of human understanding.* Probably the most crucial underlying element in this theory is its account of what is involved in having a mind. It rejects the image of the mind as an initially empty room ready to be furnished with ideas, or as a kind of organism whose features, present in a rudimentary form from birth, come to maturity through an inner-determined process of growth. What it claims, in the first place, is that concepts are not acquired by or placed in a preexisting mind, but are the constituent elements of the mind itself. Thus, to lack a certain range of concepts is, to that extent, to be lacking in mind. Second, the kinds of experiences a human being has (what he perceives, feels, imagines, wants, chooses, does) depend on his acquiring conceptual capacities. Third, although these capacities belong to individuals, and in that sense are subjective, the learning of them in most cases involves the acceptance of socially established criteria. Moreover, many of our concepts are employed as integral parts of significant common human practices such as morality, politics, law, religion, science, and art. In isolation from the public forms of understanding (including, of course, the use of language), an individual's native capacities for the development of the mind would not take him very far. Development, to any significant degree, necessarily occurs in a social and impersonal context.

At any given time, the range and quality of mind (and hence experience) that it is possible for an individual to achieve depend on the public traditions of understanding that are available to him. If these are complex, as they are in our culture, they cannot be comprehended informally, simply in the course of everyday life. They require sustained systematic effort. This is the point of having a distinct institution called "the school."

Each basic form of understanding is distinguished by some or all of the following: a set of concepts, a method of inquiry, criteria for justifying claims; a systematic body of principles, theories, and beliefs; a tradition of practice that includes both techniques and discriminating skill in their application. Some of these forms of understanding directly involve theoretical activities: mathematics, physical science, social and behavioral science, history, and philosophy. Others are embodied in practical activities: religion, morality, politics, and the arts (including literature).

It is not necessary to debate whether this list is exhaustive. The basic purpose of the educational process, so defined, is to engage the learner with all the main forms of understanding that the best human efforts have so far devised and thus to promote a full and integral development of his mind. During the stage of general education, the emphasis is not on a specialized application of what is learned, but on enlarging one's capacities for understanding and appreciation. This interpretation of schooling should not be confused with the subject-centered curriculum in which large bodies of information are acquired by dogged efforts of memorization with very little understanding. Rather, it is concerned with the concepts and principles that are most crucial for understanding, with an appreciation of the range and limitations of different conceptual perspectives and modes of inquiry, and with learning to think, feel, imagine, and act in the ways that are made possible through the public traditions of understanding.

In general, these forms of understanding do not determine the order and method of teaching and learning, or their exact organization within a curriculum. Whether a definite order is necessary for understanding in a certain case, and what concepts and principles are most significant, can be decided only by those who know thoroughly the form of knowledge in question. But whatever the process by which the learner comes to think mathematically, scientifically, and so on, the logical and epistemological features of these forms of knowledge are crucial criteria of achievement. Obviously, throughout the process the teacher himself must have these criteria in view.

On the basis of this theory, it is clear that the school has a distinctive task that should not be confused with psychotherapy or social work, that the educational process requires a carefully designed curriculum, and that the role of the teacher is critically important. We are interested here specifically in the teacher. He is seen as a personal mediator between the learner and the living human traditions that embody standards of excellence in thought, feeling, and action. He is not simply instructing but is attempting to impart a sense of judgment and style. The latter depends, more than anything else, on the setting of example and on the suggestions that occur incidentally in the context of practice. It is beyond the reach of clear-cut rules or recipes and can be achieved only by a person who is already, to some extent at least, a master.

A teacher's competence depends, in the first place, on his grasp of the public forms of knowledge that constitute or underlie what he professes to teach. If he disregards the criteria they embody, his teaching will be at least miseducative and may be a form of indoctrination or propaganda. In the second place, his competence depends on his ability to master the practical skills and the art of engaging and influencing the mental efforts of others so that they come to know, understand, appreciate, acquire skills intelligently, and so on. It also depends on his grasp of the theory that enables him to exercise his own pedagogical skills intelligently. Thus, the ideally competent teacher of, say, history needs to share to a considerable extent the skills and knowledge of a historian and a philosopher of history; and he also needs what these accomplishments by no means entail — the pedagogical skills to help others to gain a knowledge and appreciation of history and its methods, and an awareness of how the study of history fits into the complex process of educational initiation. A teacher will be able to contribute to the latter only if he has reflected philosophically on the nature of the practice in which he engages. One advantage of placing teacher training in the context of a university is that the collaboration of experts in related fields can be more easily arranged. In the training of history teachers, for example, it would be desirable to have a team that included a master teacher in the subject, a historian, and a philosopher of history.

I happen to believe that the view of education I have just discussed is the only satisfactory one when we are talking about what is done in a distinct social institution called a school, where there is a special vocational group called teachers. Those opposed to the theory often argue that a preoccupation in the school with the major public forms of knowledge and understanding is bound to have elitist consequences; that a minority has the capacity and interest to engage in this rigorous, disciplined kind of learning; and that, in the age of mass education, it is unrealistic to think that society can provide an adequate number of highly qualified teachers. Without attempting to deal with these objections thoroughly, I will make a number of summary comments.

First, if the connection between the development of the mind and the public traditions of understanding is correct, we should not too lightly make assumptions about what proportion of our society is capable of being educated in the sense we are considering (which, for convenience, I shall call liberal education). Despite all the talk about equal educational opportunity, there is a serious danger of selling people short on what they get in the name of education.

Second, rather than substitute other activities, it seems preferable to allow the learner to progress at his own rate and to the level of sophistication in the public traditions of understanding that his abilities allow. (No one ever thoroughly masters even one of these traditions.) Within the main forms of knowledge, there is considerable room for variation; a flexible arrangement will enable the predominant interests of the learner at any time to be reflected, but still within the broad framework of the common curriculum. Of course, it is precisely for average and slow learners that special pedagogical skills are most required. And until we have exhausted our ingenuity in devising effective methods, we are surely not justified in saying, "S has difficulty with educationally significant learning. Let's find some alternative to keep him occupied and happy." If attention is given to the key concepts, principles, and procedures within each form of knowledge, and to the basic connections and differences between them, the whole process of education is rendered more intelligible and the effort of learning more economical.[6]

Third, if after all reasonable efforts have been made there are still a majority unable (or unwilling) to engage in liberal education, then by all means they should be free to do something else. I see no good reason why an individual should be required to take part in any kind of schooling after about fourteen years of age. But at the same time, those who want liberal education should not be denied the opportunity. Does this leave us with an elite? For those who value such an education, the answer is obviously yes: an educated elite, but not necessarily a closed social or class elite. There are less drastic ways of preventing the latter than by repudiating the best achievements of human understanding. For example, through social reform and special educational arrangements, access to the educated elite could be given to everyone in the society who had the appropriate ability and interest; and in general, economic opportunity need depend not on having a liberal education, but on possessing the particular skills for the job. A few years ago, people became very sensitive to the dangers of a meritocracy. In our society, the dangers of mediocracy seem much more imminent and serious.

Fourth, the possibility that the system cannot supply an adequate number of suitably qualified teachers is a serious one — that is, if we assume that the objective is to provide a liberal education for most, if not all, members of society. One practical measure is to ensure that the general working conditions of teachers are such as to attract highly competent candidates. It may also be possible to reduce the extent of the problem somewhat if various tasks in or relating to the educational process can be carried out by assistant teachers and teacher aides working under the guidance of master teachers. Only the latter would need the full range of professional education to which I have referred. The use of sophisticated machines for certain aspects of teaching could further help to relieve the burden. Of course, if society in general accepts a form of schooling in which the practice of teaching does not depend on any grasp of related theory and mastery of any systematic kind of knowledge, the scale of the problem is radically changed. There would be no need to recruit particularly competent people, and the skills of the trade could be learned almost entirely on the job. At the same time, there would be a substantial saving to society in the cost of teacher education and the wages that teachers could reasonably expect.

Basic Issues in Teacher Education
Against the background of these very broad questions, let us consider briefly some issues that bear more proximately on the planning of teacher education.

The first matter concerns the degree of pluralism there might be in the training of people for work in education. It is not likely that the multipurpose character of the school will be abandoned in favor of an institution that is devoted almost exclusively to liberal education. Even if the school's role were narrowed somewhat, the prevailing interpretations of what counts as education would still admit a very broad range of activities. Given this situation, the question is whether faculties of education and teachers' colleges should themselves be multipurpose training centers. In relation to this question, I would point out that there is one kind of training, not given at present in any other tertiary institution, that teacher education institutions could provide — namely, a thorough grounding in the theory and practice of inducting children and adolescents into the main traditions of human understanding. Other agencies are already engaged in training people for the various additional tasks that are thought to have a place in the school. Thus, whether counseling, therapy, social work, and so on are thought to be adjuncts to the central purpose of schooling or to be what schooling is all about, their practitioners could be quite well trained — and without unnecessary duplication — in the relevant university departments or their equivalent. Of course, some overlap is desirable in the training programs of teachers and of therapists and others who are going to work in the schools, and this is one good reason for making the teachers' colleges a part of the university.

Even when teachers are trained in institutions that are devoted exclusively to the training of teachers, it is useful for them to offer a diversity of programs.[7] While the analogy between a hospital and a school should not be pushed too far, I think it can be reasonably argued that just as those who are involved in the central task of the hospital have different levels of training in relation to medical science and skill, so those who are involved in the more narrowly defined work of education should have different levels of teacher training in relation to educational theory and practice. As long as we are serious about trying to *educate* the whole population, the use of various kinds of teaching assistants working with master teachers is a practical necessity. It would be absurd to expect that society could provide enough master teachers (whose professional training would involve a program of four to five years at the university level) to carry on the gigantic enterprise of schooling on their own. In fact, it will be difficult enough to find an adequate number of master teachers even when there is a division of labor.[8] This problem can be alleviated somewhat if the role of school administrators is considerably simplified and reduced in significance and master teachers are given the prestige (reflected in salary) that administrators now enjoy. At any rate, assuming that various assistant teaching activities are recognized, there should be a variety of teacher training programs, differing in such matters as level of general education required for admission, length of program, and emphasis on theory.

A second basic issue arises over the relevance of theory to the work of a teacher. Despite the common rhetoric about teaching as a professional enterprise, there has been a strong anti-theoretical tendency among teachers and, sometimes, among teacher educators. Many of the anti-theorists agree that a person must know something in order to teach it. But they are inclined to suppose that knowing something well is a sufficient condition for getting others to learn it. Thus, what the teacher learned at high school or university, combined with a lot of teaching practice under the guidance of experienced teachers in the school, will suffice. Some anti-theorists will admit the need for considering a certain amount of educational theory in a piecemeal fashion if it is directly relevant to the solution of this or that specific problem in teaching practice. Others, who interpret the role of teacher as that of a therapist or social worker, are able to dispense with both content knowledge and educational theory and to reduce the whole of teacher training to on-the-job apprenticeship. Even among those who urge the importance of a thorough, theoretically based — and thus professional — program of training, there is conflict between a liberal and vocational emphasis.

What position one takes on these disputes will depend to a large extent on the answer one gives to the questions we were discussing earlier. If we assume that the present conditions of mass schooling and the law of compulsory attendance are unlikely to change, and if we further assume that the teacher is concerned in some fashion with introducing the learner to the significant forms of human understanding, I would argue that the anti-theoretical approach is probably adequate for the various kinds of teaching assistants, but is quite inadequate for the training of master teachers. And without a substantial proportion of the latter, the schools cannot provide an education of significant quality. Of course, teaching is also an art, and like any other art its practical skills are acquired through performance under the guidance of someone who is already a master of the art. No one becomes an accomplished teacher simply by knowing a lot of theory. At the same time, there are humanistic and scientific studies that provide a theoretical context for understanding and interpreting the teacher's role, and a set of methods for investigating educational problems. Ideally, the teacher should not know simply the content that he intends to teach to the learner. It is usually desirable, if not necessary, for him to possess a knowledge of the context of what he teaches (for example, the knowledge of the political and social history of a period for the teaching of its literature) and a "metalevel" understanding of the logical conditions affecting its main concepts, the kind of evidence that is relevant to justifying its claims, and the similarities and differences it has with other forms of knowledge in these respects. Hence, in the full range of teacher training there is scope for some programs that are predominantly apprenticeships and for others that emphasize a substantial range of theory (in addition to further liberal education and specialization in the area in which one is to teach).

The broad pattern of teacher training might be as follows:
1. A general introductory phase of practical preparation, from one to two years in length. There would be some differentiation to anticipate broad differences in teaching situations. Stress would be placed on the content to be taught, on practice teaching under expert guidance that focuses on the development of specific, basic teaching skills, and on careful analysis and discussion of a wide range of typical teaching situations. Theory would be introduced only in the context of questions about practice.
2. A teaching apprenticeship of about three years under the guidance of master teachers in various kinds of schools. Obviously, the effective-

ness of such a scheme would depend to a great extent on the quality and number of master teachers.

3. An advanced teacher education program of about four years. Applicants who had completed the apprenticeship would be admitted on the basis of general ability and demonstrated teaching skills. The program's length would depend on whether the candidate had done an undergraduate degree before entering phase one. The successful completion of this program would be a necessary condition for admission as a master teacher. The initial apprenticeship would probably be an adequate preparation for the work of assistant teachers.

4. A variety of in-service training programs for all teachers. Some would be taken at regular intervals and would be of a general character intended to help the teacher to update the knowledge of what he taught and to improve his practical skills. Others would provide specific training for teachers placed in a situation that was novel to them (for example, a racially mixed school, or a school in which curriculum materials are organized differently or new teaching aids are available).

In this context, a question of considerable practical importance should be raised: How are the teacher educators themselves to be trained and retrained? The placing of teacher training in a university provides no answer in itself. Programs leading to higher degrees in various disciplines, including education, are geared to preparing not teachers but researchers. The research mentality that this type of training is calculated to produce is obviously unsuitable for a task in which the primary emphasis is on applying knowledge to practice, and not on contributing to its growth. It is critically important that some graduate colleges or departments of education should provide an advanced level of training that is specifically concerned with the application of theory to the work of teacher education. Of course, there should also be changes in the salaries and working conditions of teacher education faculty, so that the higher teaching degree in education enjoys parity with the research degree.[9]

A third and final consideration is the prevalence of simplistic formulas for policy in teacher training. The theory and practice of education, perhaps even more than that of politics, tends to suffer from dogmatic fixations and slogans. I watched a television program recently in which children were shown following with rapt attention an episode of *Sesame Street*. The voice of an expert on child development was telling us that this was all rather bad because children should be active while they learn and should discover things for themselves. If *Sesame Street* has educational defects, it cannot be on account of its disregard for these narrow prescriptions for acceptable learning. Of course, "learning by doing" and "learning by discovery" have a place in educational practice, but that is a long step from supposing that they are the only desirable ways of learning. Teacher educators, above all, should have a healthy suspicion of the sloganeering and gimmickry that often go on in the name of educational research. The process of human teaching and learning is too complex to be reduced to simple formulas or metaphors.

The same point applies to suggestions about the appropriate general emphasis in the faculties of education and teachers' colleges themselves. For example, some think the quality of the personal relationship between teacher and pupils is all-important; they are primarily concerned with the "personality" of the teacher trainee and stress activities in the school that directly involve the expression of feeling. Others are preoccupied with logical operations in teaching discourse, the logical structure of the content taught, and the psychology of cognitive development in children.[10] To concentrate exclusively on either of these aspects surely betrays a radical misunderstanding of what it is to engage in education. Of course there are personal relationships in teaching and learning whose quality has a significant effect on what the participants are trying to achieve. In this, education is no different from innumerable other human activities. But the nature of education is such (at least in the interpretation I am supporting) that a distinctive kind of personal relationship between the teacher and the learner is indispensable. The process of education does not consist in the acquisition of abstract, timeless procedures and pieces of information. It is an initiation into public, communal ways of acting that express human purposes and reflect a history of immense human effort. And it proceeds through a personal exchange with those who are themselves actively engaged in such ways of acting. In Michael Oakeshott's words,

> A teacher is one in whom some part or aspect or passage of this inheritance is alive. He has something of which he is a master to impart (an ignorant teacher is a contradiction) and he has deliberated its worth and the manner in which he is to impart it to a learner whom he knows. He is himself the custodian of that "practice" in which an inheritance of human understanding survives and is perpetually renewed in being imparted to newcomers.[11]

Moreover, to be educated in the public modes of understanding is a matter of learning not simply to think in certain ways, but also to perceive, feel, imagine, and act differently. At the present time, there is probably more danger of placing the emphasis on affective experience at the expense of thought than of the converse. John Schaar and Sheldon Wolin have referred to

> the underlying agreement between the techno-scientist and the hippie, the one declaring that values are subjective preferences, the other mumbling,

"Man, I'm only doing my thing." The end result signifies that values are no longer shareable as knowledge, and hence one gets only their functional equivalents: sensation, feeling, spectacle.[12]

The curricula of the school and of the teacher education institution should be so designed and implemented as to reinforce the complex interplay among thought, feeling, and action. We need teachers who can communicate feelingly, but who also have something worth communicating.

Theories of learning in education and interpretations of the teacher's role are not simply descriptions of how things are. They reflect, at least implicitly, answers to normative questions about the nature of education and the role of the school as a social institution. In attempting to deal intelligently with conflicting claims about how children should learn and what teachers should do, we are forced back to these more general underlying questions. Although this discussion has indicated a clear personal preference, my main purpose has been to draw attention to a few salient features of the larger controversy that cannot be ignored in the planning of teacher education. Since some stand must inevitably be taken, it is better that it be done explicitly and with justifying arguments. We may find that the diversity of theories about education and the school expresses such fundamental differences of belief in our society that there is no possibility of a consensus through reasoned persuasion. If so, we should seriously reexamine our policy of maintaining what is an essentially monolithic form of public schooling and of teacher education.

NOTES

1. We are concerned here with the teachers of children and adolescents.

2. See Paul Goodman, *Compulsory Mis-education and the Community of Scholars* (New York: Random House, Vintage Books, 1964).

3. This is not equivalent to asking what role the school should play, for one could claim that the schools should be used for various purposes in addition to educating.

4. Johann Heinrich Pestalozzi, *Address to His House on the Occasion of His Seventy-Second Birthday* (January 12, 1818). Quoted in *Encyclopaedia of Religion and Ethics*, ed. by James Hastings (New York: Charles Scribner's Sons, 1914), vol. 5, p. 166. Excerpts of the Address are included in Lewis Flint Anderson, *Pestalozzi* (New York: AMS Press, 1970), pp. 127–45.

5. *Children and Their Primary Schools: A Report of the Central Advisory Council for Education (England)*, Lady Plowden, J. P., chairman (London: H.M.S.O., 1967); and *Living and Learning: The Report of the Provincial*

Committee on Aims and Objectives of Education in the Schools of Ontario, E. M. Hall and L. A. Dennis, chairmen (Toronto: Ontario Department of Education, 1968).

6. See, for example, Jerome S. Bruner, *The Process of Education* (Cambridge, Mass.: Harvard University Press, 1960), especially chap. 2.

7. See B. Othanel Smith, Saul B. Cohen, and Arthur Pearl, *Teachers for the Real World* (Washington, D.C.: American Association of Colleges for Teacher Education, 1969), chap. 3, for a discussion of diversity in teaching roles and the training appropriate for them.

8. In Ontario, there are approximately 12,500 physicians, compared with 103,650 teachers in all elementary and secondary schools and a further 7,800 full-time teachers in colleges and universities (figures for July 1971, provided by the Ontario Teachers' Federation and the Ontario Medical Association). In *Salaries and Qualifications of Teachers in Public Elementary and Secondary Schools, 1969–70* (Ottawa: Dominion Bureau of Statistics, 1971), it is reported that 13 percent of public elementary school teachers in Ontario had a university degree in 1967/68 (the latest year for which statistics from Ontario are available). Among public secondary school teachers, 7 percent had a master's or doctoral degree in the same year.

9. Compare the comments on the training of teacher educators in Smith et al., *Teachers for the Real World*, pp. 161–63.

10. These and other aspects that have recently been given preeminence in teacher training are referred to in an unpublished paper by H. S. Broudy, "The Uses and Abuses of Diversity in Teacher Education" (paper presented at the ICET Conference in Sydney, Australia, August 7–8, 1970). See also G. H. Bantock, "Conflicts of Values in Teacher Education," *The Critical Survey* (Winter 1970): 105–16.

11. Michael Oakeshott, "Education: The Engagement and Its Frustration," *Proceedings of the Philosophy of Education Society of Great Britain* (January 1971), p. 50.

12. John Schaar and Sheldon Wolin, "Education and the Technological Society," *The New York Review of Books* (October 9, 1969), p. 4.

Radical Notes

John McMurtry

Teacher education has traditionally taken the form of a tightly government-controlled, compulsory, and extended pre-job pedagogical training period (one or two years) in a special and separate institution called a teachers' college, or college or faculty of education.

This system has been so notoriously mean-spirited, oppressive, and incompetent that it does not serve much purpose to document the many complaints against it or the noxious effects it has had. Its reputation as "mickey mouse," "tyrannical," "degrading," and so on is too well known to be dwelt on here. What does deserve attention, however, is (*a*) a clear identification of the *presuppositions* upon which this system rests and (*b*) an attempt to suggest some alternatives that avoid the shortcomings of the present set-up.

"Assumption Set" of the Present System
The presuppositions of the traditional teacher education system are—
1. that there be *schools* — as opposed to, say, independent subject practitioners operating singly or in groups who provide educational services paid for through a system of free government vouchers (as in medicare and legal aid systems), or to voluntarily attended community education centers with subject consultants, learning equipment, open play and social areas, and a computer to connect learners and consultants with similar interests;
2. that there be a *full-time professional job of teacher* — as opposed to, say, teaching as an "incidental" function of interested and perhaps needy skilled people (writers, artists, scientists, doctors, lawyers, technocrats, craftsmen) who would devote a regular, publicly paid part of their day to instructing the young, or who would instruct in

return for help on the job, or who would spend a certain number of salaried weeks per year in an educational institution (with the current day-care function of teachers being given over to neighborhood day-care centers);
3. that there be *compulsory teacher education* for all those filling the role of publicly paid teachers — as opposed to, say, such education being an open matter to be decided upon by aspiring or practicing teachers at any time, whether at the behest of their boards, their schools, or their pupils, or according to their personal desires;
4. that teacher education take place in *an institution separated from the schools* — as opposed to its taking place through, say, an intern system, where the candidate combines work for one or two years as a paid teaching intern in a regular school with a flexible program of university courses in the philosophy of education, sociology of education, psychology, and similar subjects;
5. that teacher education be essentially confined to a one- or two-year *terminal preprofessional period* — as opposed to its being, say, a series of shorter programs taken periodically over a number of teaching years that would be substantiated by "education shelves" (journals and classic works) in every staffroom, by regular school seminars and teach-ins on education, and by the real involvement of classroom teachers in educational decision making;
6. that teacher education be *under the control of a provincial government department* — as opposed to its being under the control of the universities alone (as is beginning to occur now), or the teaching profession itself, or individual boards or schools.

Now this cluster of presuppositions of the traditional teacher education system does not seem (as my sketchily articulated alternatives indicate) at all defensible on purely educational grounds. It may well serve to protect the license-property of the teaching profession, various other educational monopolies and interests, and the maintenance of the schools as cultural police stations; but it seems quite unjustifiable on the grounds of promoting the psychical growth of the young. Indeed, there does not appear to be any body of official or unofficial evidence to support the holding of any one of the six presuppositions as educationally valid.

If it is true that this set of assumptions of the teacher education system is *unjustifiable* on educational grounds, but *functional* for the preservation of certain interests of the pedagogical estate as well as the general maintenance of culture control, then we are confronted with a choice. Either we opt for a new system that *is* justifiable on educational grounds, or we stick with the old system, which preserves uneducational or even anti-educational structures. Or — the more subtle choice — we plump for something in between. Although I cannot help viewing such compromises as the latter with suspicion, I will attempt to sketch just such a solution.

Proposed Renovation of the System
Here is the suggestion:
1. Remove *all* Ministry of Education control over teacher education programs (control the Ministry already claims to be willing to relinquish).
2. Leave the teachers' colleges and colleges of education largely unchanged, but have them administered individually by a governing council of volunteer staff and an equal number of elected students.
3. Where the teacher education institution is in the vicinity of a university, arrange cross-appointments of university faculty to provide a series of definitive lectures on the philosophy of education, the sociology of education, educational psychology, and so on, to the college as a whole. Where the teacher education institution is not in the vicinity of a university, hire university-qualified staff in some or all of the areas mentioned to form an interdisciplinary department inside the teachers' college.
4. As a phasing-in licensing alternative to formal teacher education, allow a reasonably paid internship period inside a large set of regular schools. These schools would be dispersed throughout the province (say, one to each county board) and would contain in each case a cross-appointed or permanent interdisciplinary department similar to that described in (3).
5. Adopt the following ad hoc measures —
   a) make $100-a-year staffroom shelves of education journals and classics (to be selected by the staff) an obligatory component of every school;
   b) allow a certain increasing percentage (starting at, say, 5 percent) of the staff of all schools to be unlicensed, with their only qualification for entry being that they have a professional or distinguished background in one of the arts or sciences;
   c) start democratizing and opening up the schools themselves, so that teachers have the freedom to experiment and the responsibility of decision making that are presently denied to them but that are necessary conditions of all education, teacher or otherwise;
   d) make provision for a strong student voice in the way classes are conducted (such as having students vote on learning procedures or evaluate their teachers at the end of the course), so that those most acquainted with teaching performance are able to make their views effectively known to the practicing teacher.

None of these proposals are so threatening to vested interest or cultural control that they cannot be accepted. And their implementation would significantly improve the teacher education situation. Of course, pressed to present a more fundamental solution — all established interests aside — I would end all present formal pedagogical training. Qualification requirements and selection of teachers should be entirely in the hands of democratically run community education centers, a role that the schools should fill.

Afterword

It would be wrong to end an article on teacher education without offering a concept of a teacher. There are many such concepts, but they all imply a *student*. Thus, when we seek a concept of a teacher, it is probably more instructive to think in terms of the teacher–student pair than of the teacher alone — that is, in terms of a *relationship*.

Three concepts of the teacher–student relationship can be offered that more or less cover the field: master–servant, professional–client, and I–thou.

The teacher–student concept that obtains *in fact* in our traditional education institutions is that of the teacher as master and the student as servant. The teacher dictates work tasks, enforces standards, makes deadlines, controls speech, sets the rules of behavior, judges performance, writes references, and — this is the linchpin of the mechanism of control — owns the power to exclude the student from the work place and, thus, the material means of life. The student is, of course, on the receiving end of all these forms of power. He performs the required work tasks, obeys the standards, meets the deadlines, conforms to the imposed rules of speech and behavior, and so forth; and he is, throughout, under the hidden or overt threat of being excluded (suspended, expelled, failed) from his present and even future employment if he does not so serve. In some cases, namely, in most primary and secondary schools, this structure of domination actually verges on a jailer–prisoner relationship, as the language of these schools suggests ("patrol," "detention," "term," "corporal punishment," "incorrigible," "squealed," "correction," "confess," "outside world," "offender"). In short, the relationship is one of domination and servitude, intractably enshrined as such by virtue of the master's (the teacher's) being *obliged*, by written regulation, to impose his set of institutional powers on his charges. If he fails to do so, he will be excluded from his life-support base by higher authority *himself*.

The second concept of the teacher–student relationship, professional–client, is the one of educationist rhetoric and pretense — that is, of educationist *ideology*. Teachers make a very conscientious effort to gain public (and their own) acceptance of this ideological concept by continually talking about "professionals," "professionalism," "the teaching profession," and so on. They do this even though the necessary conditions of a profession — voluntary clientele and self-government — are explicitly absent (except in the case of university teachers, who represent a curious mix of master and professional). Educators seldom call students "clients," but there is an increasing tendency to treat them like, for example, medical patients who have to undergo modifying operations before they can be released (from the schools) as certified safe-and-well members of society. There is a certain confusion in this whole concept, as one might expect given its considerable conflict with reality. But it is one that is very widely employed and implied in educationese, and one that has impelled an increasing movement toward changing teachers into independent practitioners and students into voluntary clientele, with rights of free-market purchase by means of an educational version of an OHIP card (a voucher).

It may well be that this second concept of the teacher–student relationship will eventually go beyond rhetoric and take actual hold in our educational practice in place of the master–servant principle. But this is unlikely to happen, in the near future, inasmuch as the overriding social function of the schools — however it may be dressed up — is to produce obedient youth who will submit by habit to the internal dictatorship of current corporate bureaucracies, families, and labor lines. The undermining of the crucial master–servant conditioning of the schools by granting students the status of clients with freedom of choice seems too obviously subversive to vested ruling powers to be tolerated in our society yet.

The final concept of the teacher–student relationship, I–thou, is what might be called an *ideal*, realized neither in practice nor even in the ideology of educators generally. It has a long history, however, stretching from the bodhisattvas of Buddhism to the modern advocates of radical free schools. With this concept, both teacher and student are construed as autonomous subjects. Unlike the master–servant relationship, there exists no right of command or obligation to command on the part of the teacher. And unlike the professional–client relationship, the student is not confined in his identity to the role of a client to be serviced, for a fee, in a one-directional, specific, and prescribed way. Rather, the relationship is one of human ends-in-selves meeting in mutually committed encounter. The teacher is simply he who has the authority — and only the authority — of craft and experienced interest; an authority that can shift spontaneously with the locus of discourse (for example, I have much to say to my students about philosophy and literature, but they have taught me much about underground music and the values of their generation). The relationship is nondirective, it is two-way, and it is mutually concerned and creative. It is, in brief, a form of love.

What is most disturbing about our present educational institutions — what indeed keeps us perpetually on the verge of quitting altogether — is that this "ideal" relationship of teacher and student is, through a myriad of impersonal administrative dictates, *forbidden*. It is, as it were, against the law. That this should be the case in the one place in our society that is putatively dedicated to the growth of minds rather than profits and things is the unkindest cut of all. We require, I fear, a revolutionary change of vision in such things, or we are lost.

How Not to Reform a Teacher Education System: Ontario 1966-1971

Douglas Myers and David Saul

On August 19, 1971, the Minister of Education for Ontario, Robert Welch, publicly acknowledged the failure of an important government education policy. That was not, of course, quite the way he put it at the time, nor was it what the press noticed. The major emphasis in Welch's statement was on the announcement of an agreement, just concluded between his department and York University, putting Lakeshore Teachers' College under the control of York and establishing a university faculty of education there. Almost by way of an aside, however, the Minister also mentioned that all further negotiations between the Department of Education and a number of Ontario universities regarding the fate of eight other government-run teacher training colleges would be suspended "until there is a review."[1] Although this was in an important sense by far the more significant part of the announcement, Mr. Welch could perhaps be forgiven a certain decent reticence, for, in effect, he was giving an unceremonious hoist to a policy inaugurated with considerable fanfare five years earlier by his predecessor, now the Premier, William Davis.

In March 1966, Davis had told the legislature that the government was embarking on a teacher education policy that would result in the transfer to Ontario's universities of the major responsibility for preparing teachers for the province's elementary, as well as its secondary, schools.[2] Although the Minister was careful to caution that "sweeping changes in teacher education cannot be made overnight,"[3] he was obviously optimistic that swift progress could be made in implementing this important policy. Nor was he less sanguine the following year when he delivered a progress report to the legislature. He described the policy as "the most significant development in teacher education in Ontario in this century," a development he felt would have a great and positive impact on the quality of education Ontario would be able to provide for its young people; and although he again acknowledged the difficulties involved, he was "very delighted with the reaction of the universities" and was "hopeful that [the teachers' colleges] could be fully integrated by the early 1970's."[4]

Although William Davis seems a man not much given to wild despair over the mistakes of the past, one may suppose that he felt some dismay in August 1971 as he surveyed the shambles his government's bold teacher education policy had become. Over a five-year period, the Department of Education had managed to negotiate and sign agreements with only five universities for the transfer of teachers' colleges,[5] and the development and implementation of new programs at those institutions was at a very embryonic stage indeed. At least as significant as the completed negotiations were the omissions from the list. No agreements had been reached with a number of major universities — Western, McMaster, Toronto, Queen's, and Carleton — and no provision had been arranged with Laurentian University for Sudbury and North Bay.

In the meantime, other events and developments had overtaken the government by 1971. Education was no longer regarded as the panacea for all social ills — though what would take its place was not yet clear — and the great spending spree of the 1960s was over. School enrollment was declining, and the perennial teacher shortage had become, almost overnight it seemed, the teacher surplus problem. Politicians were beginning to respond to increasing public concern about rising education costs at all levels. Thus, under the circumstances, Robert Welch's decision to suspend teacher education negotiations with the universities and to review the entire situation seemed eminently sensible.

Departmental officials have been heard to observe since that it was fortunate that the negotiations had gone so slowly after 1966 and that more university faculties of education had not been established. In view of the altered circumstances of the early 1970s, perhaps they are right; but the fact remains that the government's intended policy failed, and the province found itself, in 1971, stuck precisely in midstream, with eight universities involved in teacher education and eight government teachers' colleges still functioning. What, then, went wrong? Students of the history of Ontario education will have to await the appearance of a number of memoirs and private papers before a full and detailed account can be written. It is possible, however, to unravel enough of the strands to present the main outline of the story. It is a saga from which neither of the major protagonists — the government on one side and the universities on the other — emerges with much credit.

The MacLeod Report

The tale begins with the Minister's Committee on the Training of Elementary School Teachers (the MacLeod Committee), which reported in March 1966 after two years of hearings, study, and discussion.[6] As one observer put it, "Ontario has never been noted for the importance it has placed on the formal preparation of its elementary school teachers."[7] The establishment of the MacLeod Committee was official recognition that some fundamental changes had to be made in order to improve what was almost universally recognized to be a very unsatisfactory training system for those teachers.

Among the committee's forty-seven recommendations, the most important was that the Department of Education should continue to certify teachers, but that the programs for all teacher education in Ontario, both elementary and secondary, should be provided by the university. These programs should extend over at least four years and should combine roughly 75 percent liberal arts, natural sciences, or social sciences with 25 percent professional studies and training. The programs would be organized in two basic types of plan: either three or four years of academic undergraduate work for a B.A. followed by a year of teacher training for a B.Ed. (commonly referred to as a *consecutive* plan), or four or five years of joint academic and professional studies leading to a B.A./B.Ed. (commonly referred to as a *concurrent* plan). In the view of the committee, the transfer should proceed as quickly as possible, through a series of formal bilateral agreements between the Department and the universities concerned. The committee was at pains to emphasize the necessity for recognizing each university's autonomy. Separate agreements would maintain "flexibility of programs." Each "agreement should indicate clearly the areas of responsibility charged to the university and the authority delegated to it for the purpose of discharging its responsibilities."[8] At the same time, the committee urged the establishment of an implementation committee "with representation from the universities . . . to study and implement, step by step, the proposals" it had recommended. The implementation committee also would provide a "continuing review of the changing situation year by year. . . ."[9]

These, then, were the major suggestions of the MacLeod Committee for the reorganization and improvement of teacher education in Ontario. "The Department and the Minister are in complete agreement with the general program suggested," Davis declared when tabling the report in March 1966, "and it will be the policy of my department to implement plans to this end as quickly as possible."[10] Immediately, departmental officials set to work to draw up a specific policy on integration, and visits were made to each of the universities concerned to discuss the MacLeod recommendations and the terms of the transfer of each teachers' college. Significantly, however, the Department made no move to establish an implementation committee or other such body. A year later, Davis reported substantial progress, reviewed the situation at each university concerned in generally favorable terms, and predicted that the first agreement would be signed by July 1, 1968, and that two more might also be ready at that time.[11]

In reality, the difficulties in reaching agreements with the universities were to prove much more substantial than the government in 1967 either realized or at any rate was prepared to admit. Opposition spokesmen expressed some reservations about the ease and the significance of the progress the Minister claimed was being made. The Liberal leader, Robert Nixon, pointed out that despite the long-time location of secondary colleges of education on campus, they remained "very much separated from the main stream of university life" and seemed to have "very little of the atmosphere of academic freedom or development that is normally associated in the university." Stephen Lewis of the New Democrats observed that Davis's assessment of university cooperation "would seem to imply that the Brahmins are lowering the gates as it were; that the bridge over the moat is coming down, that mere mortals are being allowed into the palace."[12] Lewis did not seem convinced; and, indeed, events were to reveal that the skepticism of the opposition was more justified than the optimism of the government.

The University and Teacher Education
It is perhaps helpful in an examination of the recent history of teacher education in Ontario to take note of the general context of government–university relations in which it is set. As the Wright Report, and the reaction to it, make clear, Ontario is going through a period of reassessing and readjusting the complex and frequently contentious relationship between the government and the universities.[13] The same process is also occurring in other parts of Canada, in Britain, and in the United States. On the one hand stands the government, the legitimate guardian of the public interest, but possessed of a bureaucratic momentum that often works against that interest; on the other stand the universities, champions of a proud tradition of individual and intellectual independence whose behavior as privileged, expensive, and socially influential institutions often fails to match the rhetoric of their ideals. Neither has a corner on virtue. Out of this current reassessment of the role of the university and its relations with society, some new balance of control and autonomy seems likely to emerge. The attempt to reorganize Ontario teacher education has taken place in the midst of this wider reexamination and, indeed, serves

to illuminate some of the peculiar tensions and problems that exist between the government and the university.

The involvement of Ontario universities in the training of *secondary* school teachers, which goes back to the early years of this century, has never been a simple or easy one. Faculties of education were first established at the University of Toronto and at Queen's in 1907, but were discontinued in 1920 because they had proved unsuccessful. They were replaced by the Ontario College of Education (O.C.E.), at the University of Toronto, which retained a monopoly position until the 1960s. Relations between O.C.E. and the university seem to have ranged from distant to hostile during most of this period. The terms of the 1920 agreement that established O.C.E. gave the Minister of Education wide-ranging and final powers. To its critics, the agreement gave the distinct impression that "the association with the university was merely a matter of departmental convenience and left the university with no real influence over the program." Matters came to a head in the 1950s, when the Minister of Education ignored all the usual university procedures and parachuted his own candidate into the deanship of the college. This very nearly resulted in a complete breach between the university and the government, and it certainly made the position of the college and its staff very difficult. As Fleming puts it, "The atmosphere from that time on was naturally extremely chilly, and the college was pushed further into isolation."[14]

Nor was the problem resolved when a second college of education was established at the University of Western Ontario in 1963. As at the University of Toronto, the terms of the agreement between the government and the University of Western Ontario left the ownership of the lands and buildings at Althouse College and all the important final powers in terms of staffing, programs, and so on, in the hands of the Department of Education. Fleming dryly comments, "The fact that all of an institution's physical assets were under government ownership did not help to create the impression that it was an integral part of a university."[15]

Only with the establishment of McArthur College of Education at Queen's in 1965 was there evidence that a more satisfactory blend of control and independence might be achieved. The terms of the agreement still gave the Department ownership, but pains were taken in a number of clauses to make it explicit that, although the Minister should retain the right to certify teachers and should be consulted on matters of joint concern, the university must be granted the widest possible discretion in operating the college as an integral part of its community. Subsequently, a revised agreement between the government and university was signed at Toronto in 1966 that, among other things, gave the university ownership. In summary, it would seem safe to say that a basis exists at all three universities upon which closer relations between the faculty of education and the rest of the university may develop, but at the moment the faculties remain somewhat on the periphery of university life.

The difficulties and tensions outlined above not only illustrate that the task of truly integrating teacher education into the university is a formidable one, but also raise the question of whether the university is the most appropriate setting for the education and training of teachers. The evidence that it is, is far from conclusive. The rationale usually advanced begins with the unobjectionable contention that an advanced level of personal education is a desirable quality for a teacher to possess. It is further argued that, compared to, say, entering teacher training straight from secondary school graduation, spending several years at the university adds significantly to the student's maturity and judgment. This too seems a sensible notion, although, of course, there are many experiences other than university that also would result in an individual's acquiring at least as much maturity and judgment. There is no doubt, however — and this has been a compelling motivation for teachers themselves — that the possession of a university degree has traditionally increased one's status in relation to other "professional" occupations and in the community at large.

Beyond these factors, the ultimate justification for locating teacher education in a university rests on the conviction that the university provides a setting and an atmosphere in which fundamental issues can be examined critically, fresh alternatives can be explored, and promising, imaginative programs can be developed. It is precisely at this crucial point, however, that the serious doubts arise. Although it is clear that the conservative, bureaucratic, closely controlled atmosphere that for so long characterized the teachers' colleges was inimical to critical thinking, individual excellence, and program experimentation, it is far from certain that the universities are capable of doing much better.[16]

Universities have been and still are deeply ambivalent about teaching. They are teaching institutions, but they pay very little attention to the process of teaching. University professors tend to be highly critical of the quality of teaching in the elementary and secondary schools and of the preparation of the students who qualify for university, but they are also extremely wary — if not contemptuous — of conscious considerations of methodology and teaching technique. For the most part, they do as they were done to — giving lectures, seminars, tutorials, term papers — and generally operate on the comforting assumption that if an individual "knows" a great deal about something, he will surely apply that knowledge effectively. The university itself, however, provides plenty of examples of the fact that splendid scholars do not necessarily make splendid teachers.

Other considerations also raise serious questions about the universities' capacity to improve significantly the quality of teacher education in Ontario. This province's universities have traditionally taken a narrow, rather rigid, discipline-oriented approach to knowledge. Such an approach has meshed rather well with the secondary school system, but it clearly requires drastic modification when applied to elementary education. Moreover, even with greatly expanded enrollment, the university has never had to deal directly with the problems of mass education in the way the elementary and to a lesser extent the secondary schools must. In view of all this, it is perhaps not surprising that the education of secondary school teachers has never been accorded a secure or honored place in the university community in Ontario. Rather, it has been segregated into a separate year, following the completion of undergraduate studies, and isolated in a building on the extreme edge of the campus.

Lest this picture seem too bleak and pessimistic, it must be noted that the 1960s were for Ontario universities a period of unprecedented self-criticism and upheaval. As a result, a good deal of the uncompromising confidence of the university in its own role, procedures, and curriculum has been severely shaken and modified, and there is considerable indication that the university may be prepared to consider seriously the fundamental problems and implications of teacher education in a way that would not have been possible a decade ago. At any rate, it was clearly the hope of the MacLeod Committee that its recommendations would not result simply in the transfer of existing programs into the universities, but would allow and encourage experimentation, diversity, and improved quality.

Contentious Issues
Even a cursory glance at the history of secondary teacher education in Ontario would have served as a warning of the difficulties involved merely in locating teacher education on the university campus, let alone in integrating it into the university's program and style. On the basis of past experience, there was little reason to suppose that the task could be accomplished smoothly and easily. On the contrary, departmental officials and university personnel had every reason to approach each other warily. If anything significant was to result from the transfer of responsibility, it might have seemed advisable at the outset to acknowledge the serious difficulties, the historic tensions, the differences in attitudes, and the vexed problems of financial and program control that existed, and to establish

a forum and procedures through which hard, but eventually productive, discussions might proceed. Such a course of action, indeed, may have been envisioned by the MacLeod Committee in its recommendation for the establishment of an implementation committee, a recommendation ignored by the government. Instead the government seems to have decided on a course that combined sunny public declarations of positive thinking with stealthy, tough, behind-the-scene bargaining with individual — and usually fledgling — universities. Initially, the collective inactivity of the university presidents encouraged the government's illusion that real progress was being made.

It was inevitable that this illusion eventually would be shattered, because the Department of Education demanded conditions that the universities were bound to challenge and resist. For one thing, the government rejected any organizational arrangement in the university other than a full college or faculty of education; a department of education within a faculty of arts, for example, would not do. In terms of program, too, the government seemed to have a clear preference. In Ontario, the *only* type of university teacher education pattern that had ever been followed was the consecutive plan. The concurrent plan, which the MacLeod Committee had recommended also, was widely regarded in university and secondary education circles as an American or western Canadian aberration, bound to be inferior because it muddied the pure water of academic study with the sludge of professional preparation.[17] Others, however, regarded this view as being as much an elitist prejudice as an objective truth. They had long felt that combined academic and professional studies might benefit both, and even went so far as to view with approval some of the teacher education programs under way to the south and to the west. The MacLeod Committee took the position that "no one pattern of professional education has proved to be the most effective," and that, in the interests of innovation and experiment in teacher education, the new faculties or colleges "should have considerable freedom and flexibility to develop distinctive programs."[18] It recommended both types, but clearly hoped that some strong concurrent plans would be developed. In his statement in the legislature in 1967, William Davis seemed to go beyond this by emphasizing that, in his view, the major recommendations of the MacLeod Report were "the transfer of teacher training to the universities and the provision of *concurrent* courses" (our emphasis).[19] Such an interpretation was certain to meet with hostility from some of the universities involved. It is not clear to what extent the Department pressed this view in its negotiations. Of the five agreements reached by 1971, only two — those with Lakehead and York universities — provided for concurrent programs, although Ottawa, Windsor, and Brock have moved in that direction since. Certainly both Carleton and McMaster initially advocated consecutive programs, which may explain the Department's lack of interest in pursuing negotiations with them. More recently, the senates of both these universities have come to favor concurrency. In any case, one might sympathize with the Department's aim but still question its strategy.[20]

What proved to be even more contentious than the Department's stand on concurrency was its attitude toward the status of the staff of the existing teachers' colleges and the qualifications appropriate for faculty in the new teacher education faculties. The MacLeod Committee had emphasized two essential qualifications: first, evidence of scholarship, which was essential "if the education faculty is to stand as an equal member in the university community"; second, and of equal and complementary importance, evidence of "distinguished and successful" teaching experience.[21] The committee had made clear its view that the Department should take the responsibility for ensuring that "any staff member of an existing Teachers' College either be placed on the staff of a faculty of education or be assured of another position in education yielding a comparable salary" — although it obviously thought that a sizable proportion of the existing staff of the teachers' colleges would be eligible for appointment to the new faculties since it noted elsewhere that "over sixty per cent of the present staff of the Teachers' Colleges possess additional or post-graduate degrees."[22] But of the 384 members of the academic staff of the colleges in 1968/69, only two had degrees beyond the master's level, and a good many of the master's degrees were M.Ed.s rather than M.A.s. Clearly, since Ph.D.s who have had wide experience in elementary and secondary teaching, plus a smattering of curriculum development, guidance, and school administration, have never been thick on the ground, it was going to be a very delicate and difficult task to establish the right blend of academic and professional criteria and a set of procedures that would be both effective in selecting the best kind of teacher education personnel and fair to all the individuals and groups concerned.

In its initial negotiations with the universities, the Department apparently proceeded on the assumption that a basic condition of amalgamation would be the virtually total permanent transfer of each teachers' college staff into the university's teacher education faculty. The available evidence suggests that the Department saw no need for any special selection procedures and believed that all teachers' college personnel should be automatically acceptable to the universities. No mention seems to have been made by the Department of procedures or criteria that might be used by the university either before or after an amalgamation to evaluate and select teachers' college personnel. And in the legislature, Davis pledged that the salaries, pensions, and other benefits of the teachers' college staff would be protected "in the transfer to the university staffs."[23] The proposed agreement with Lakehead University, for example, contained no provision for review, evaluation, or selection. Moreover, during the course of the negotiations, the Department also seems to have assumed that the principals of the teachers' colleges would become the heads of the university teacher education units. It initially rejected a suggestion that members of the staff of a teachers' college might be designated as "special lecturers" within the university in cases where they lacked the usual academic qualifications.

This position of the Department naturally raised some fundamental questions from the university's point of view. For one thing, such a mass transfer would entirely bypass the university's established procedures for the selection and appointment of staff. This would be of concern under any circumstances, but was particularly so in a case where the individuals being transferred had fewer or different academic qualifications than was usual. The situation was further complicated by the fact that many members of the staff of the teachers' colleges were receiving higher salaries than those of middle-ranking university professors. The basic issues that emerged therefore focused on faculty rank, salary, and tenure.

The Lakehead Controversy

It was precisely upon these grounds that the faculty association at Lakehead University first raised the objections that brought to an abrupt halt the negotiations with whose progress William Davis had expressed such satisfaction. The faculty association reacted strenuously against the "Proposed Memorandum of Agreement between the Province of Ontario and Lakehead University for the Establishment of a Faculty of Education at Lakehead University" when it was made public in May 1967. The agreement committed the university to a number of specific undertakings regarding admission standards, the length of term, program content, and the complete acceptance of the entire teachers' college staff into the university *without reservation*. The agreement further specified that the standards and fringe benefits of the teachers' college staff were to be maintained, but no mention whatsoever was made of academic ranking, selection, or tenure procedures. Lakehead's faculty association immediately took steps to alert the Ontario Confederation of University Faculty Associations (OCUFA) to the impending threat. In OCUFA's view, the terms of the Lakehead agreement were not only "potentially dangerous" but also "in essential contradiction to the recommendations of the MacLeod Report, particularly with respect to the conditions of faculty transferral." Accordingly OCUFA established a standing committee to study the situation and, in December 1967, adopted a set of five basic principles upon which amalgamation should take place. Four of these principles emphasized the autonomy of each university's senate to approve the terms of amalgamation and to control all matters of curriculum, degree programs, organizational structures, entrance requirements, and faculty appointments, "in particular, the selection of faculty to be transferred from a College to the University." The fifth principle declared OCUFA's opposition to staff transferral "on any basis that does not recognize that equally qualified professors should receive equal pay and rank."[24]

It seems to have been only with the eruption of the Lakehead controversy and the intervention of OCUFA that the universities — as represented by their newly formed official organization, the Committee of Presidents of Universities of Ontario (CPUO) — realized that they had, in fact, *no* overall policy on the amalgamation of the teachers' colleges. Though CPUO had set up a subcommittee in the spring of 1966 to develop recommendations on the subject, this body apparently remained inactive for over a year. By that time, of course, the Department was close to signing bilateral agreements with several universities. Had the terms of those agreements been generally known, it seems likely that some Ontario universities would have raised strong objections. As OCUFA was quick to point out, the Department did not seem to have "encouraged the implementation" of plans presented to it by such universities as York, Western, McMaster, and Trent, which had taken initiatives on the subject. Instead it had concentrated its efforts on concluding agreements, on terms it apparently considered more desirable, with Lakehead, Brock, and Laurentian.[25]

The available evidence indeed does suggest that any university that was not prepared to accept the Department's terms received a distinctly cold shoulder. A case in point was York University in Toronto. In 1965, York presented a brief to the MacLeod Committee in which it proposed an experimental, integrated concurrent teacher education program.[26] The university, however, heard nothing from the Department after the announcement of the new teacher education policy in 1966. In April 1968, York wrote the Minister of Education again, indicating its interest in the subject and expressing concern at the lack of official response. This initiative did prompt a reply from the Deputy Minister, J. R. McCarthy, in June 1968. The Department's intentions that he outlined, however, were rejected as unacceptable by the York Senate. Subsequently, a statement of principles was formulated, and on March 27, 1969, it was adopted by the York Senate. The statement, titled "Principles to Govern the Establishment of Education at York University," emphasized the close concurrent integration of education students with the undergraduate academic work of the arts and science faculties and the control, by the York Senate, of curriculum and staffing criteria and procedures.[27] Further lengthy negotiations finally resulted in agreement between York and the Department of Education in August 1971.

At any rate, given some breathing space by the breakdown of the negotiations at Lakehead in the spring of 1967, the CPUO subcommittee belatedly met with Department of Education officials in September of that year in order to "explore the common principles that should underline and inform every agreement for the integration of a program of teacher education into a university." It also established a drafting committee to prepare a statement of the "essential conditions" for a satisfactory agreement between a university and the government.[28]

Seven months later, in March 1968, two full years after the tabling of the MacLeod Report, the CPUO draft agreement proposal was forwarded to the Minister of Education. The emphasis in this document was very much on the independence and freedom of action of the university, with some appropriate concessions to the government regarding such matters as departmental control of certification, establishment of a representative advisory committee to assist in developing a program, and joint university/ministerial consultation about the initial appointment of the "academic head of the teacher education unit."[29] Autonomous university control was asserted in terms of the ownership of the land and buildings, the standards for admitting and evaluating students, the nature of the organizational structure (college/faculty/department), and the nature of the program (consecutive or concurrent). On the painful question of the transfer of staff, the presidents' proposal was rather vague but seemed to suggest some kind of initial selection of those who would join the university faculty:

> During a transitional period after the transfer of responsibility for teacher education from a teachers' college to a university, which might be envisaged as lasting three years, special arrangements will be in effect with regard to staff transferred to the university from a teachers' college. Such staff members will be encouraged to take study leave to improve their academic qualifications, and it is hoped that financial support will be provided for this purpose. The universities and the Department of Education are expected to undertake to discover alternative openings for members of the staff of a teachers' college *who for one reason or another do not join the university staff*. [Our emphasis.][30]

By late 1967, then, the main parties to the amalgamation battle were in the field with declared positions: the faculty associations and the Department were in most direct conflict; the university presidents were attempting to dig in somewhere between. Despite the opposition that had sprung up, the government seemed to be in no mood to compromise. With several universities apparently ready to sign on terms similar to those of the proposed Lakehead agreement, it could afford to wait and see.

Two other groups were also vitally concerned with the amalgamation controversy and deserve mention — the staffs of the teachers' colleges and the deans of arts and science of the universities. The teachers' college staffs were represented by the Ontario Teachers' College Association (OTCA), but they were hindered by their civil service status from taking very active or public initiatives. Doubtless OTCA made some representations to the Department, and generally it seemed to support the government's position. Throughout, however, it did not have the power to influence significantly the events that affected its members so vitally. More influential, though mainly on an individual rather than a collective basis, were the members of the Committee (latterly the Council) of Deans of Arts and Science of the Ontario universities (CDAS). Like the university presidents, the deans only began to meet on a regular basis in the mid-1960s. Although they did establish a subcommittee in October of 1966 to study the implications of the new teacher education policy, the deans generally seemed to act through the Committee of Presidents, whose increasing resistance to the Department's position they strongly supported. On at least one occasion, however, CDAS sent a letter directly to Mr. Davis "emphasizing the concern of all the Deans that university autonomy be respected in all matters pertaining to the introduction of teacher education into the universities."[31] Presumably the deans were not reticent in expressing this concern to the presidents of their respective universities.

Agreement and Aftermath

The subsequent negotiations were characterized by neither haste nor good feeling. After several meetings with the Department during the spring of 1968, the CPUO subcommittee submitted a revised statement of principles on July 17. Point eight of this statement took the position that the "staffs of the teachers' college should follow the same procedures as now apply in the case of virtually all academic appointments" and that "the universities should not be required to tie academic rank to salary and experience." The considerable hardening of the universities' attitude was illustrated by the statement's concluding paragraph:

> The integrating process should be regarded not as a transfer or transplanting, of an existing mechanism, but rather as an entirely new undertaking within the university. There would be no point in arranging transplants

which the system would reject; we ought not to contemplate a teaching enterprise which is out of line with the interests of the students (who may turn out to be much more tough minded than their predecessors).[32]

Perhaps because of the rather uncompromising, not to say undiplomatic, tone of this parting shot, the Department did not respond officially to the document for five months.

When at last a response came, however, the Department seemed to have made a slight concession. Though still insisting upon total initial transfer, it proposed a two-year period during which the university would decide whether or not it wished to retain each staff member. If it did not, the individual would have two additional years during which to find alternative employment. But that was far from enough to satisfy the CPUO subcommittee by this point, and even less the OCUFA representatives with whom it consulted.

In an attempt to break this stalemate, the presidents established a new negotiating team headed by John J. Deutsch of Queen's University. Perhaps because of Deutsch's firm belief that the amalgamation "was a good thing in principle,"[33] the reopened negotiations, after an unpromising beginning, began to make some progress. After a series of meetings through December and the first two months of the new year, and several revisions of the statement of principles, general agreement was reached. On March 14, 1969, almost three years after the announcement of the Davis teacher education policy, a "memorandum of understanding" was made public.

Like a ceasefire agreement at the end of a lengthy and inconclusive conflict, the memorandum of understanding appeared to give something to all the parties involved, at the same time leaving several issues to be resolved by further negotiation. The Department of Education seemed to have made the most substantial concessions. While acknowledging the responsibility of the Minister for certification and the need for close consultation with the Department on a number of matters, the document stressed the independence of the university in the areas of curriculum, program, organization, and staffing.[34] In comparison with the proposed Lakehead agreement, the universities had recovered a good deal of lost ground.

But the university position was not as well fortified as OCUFA had advocated. Although the authority of the university was reasserted in terms of selecting and evaluating its staff, the process would occur after, rather than prior to, its amalgamation with a teachers' college. That is to say, all staff members of the teachers' college who wished to do so would initially become members of the university teacher education organization. They would be guaranteed their existing salaries, rates of increment, and fringe benefits, and would be given the opportunity to "enhance their academic qualifications," with the Department contributing financially to their study leaves. If the university decided not to grant tenure to an individual, notice of this decision was to be given at the end of three years' service, and a further year's employment was to be guaranteed to allow the individual to find an alternative position.[35]

The Committee of Presidents called the achievement of an agreement a "decisive step towards implementing the recommendations of the MacLeod Report" and declared hopefully, "It is now open to any university in Ontario to enter into negotiations with the Department of Education with a view to assuming responsibility for a teachers' college."[36] But the damage done by three years' wrangling had been considerable.

The most serious consequence was that the basic point of the integration policy — the improvement of teacher education — got lost, or at least set aside, in the struggle. This is not to say that the issues in dispute were trivial. On the contrary, some satisfactory resolution of the fundamental problem of balancing government responsibility and university independence was an essential prerequisite to the implementation of that policy. But the controversy was so lengthy, bitter, and demoralizing to all concerned that the enthusiasm, energy, and good will necessary to undertake the difficult task of attempting to develop better ways of educating and training teachers was severely, perhaps critically, undermined.

On the available evidence at this time, the Department of Education seems to have been primarily responsible for creating this unfortunate situation. It seems highly unlikely that the Department was entirely unaware of the objections that some universities at least would have to its terms (see the York example cited). Assuming that it had an overall policy, along the lines suggested above, that policy seems to have been extremely ill conceived. In attempting to transfer the elementary teacher education system, virtually unchanged and entire, into the universities, the Department either failed to grasp the complexities of university/governmental relations or else it simply dismissed them. As eventually became clear, such an approach could not have been better designed to create suspicion and hostility among the parties involved. By attempting to proceed directly to separate, bilateral agreements, without at the same time following the MacLeod Report's recommendation for an implementation committee where issues of general concern could have been considered, the Department eliminated the possibility of reaching overall guidelines in a cooperative rather than a combative manner. Moreover, even if the Department had succeeded in getting rid of the burden of teacher education on its own terms, the result would not have been the diversity, innovation, and improved quality of teacher preparation that the MacLeod Committee had seen as essential. It is, of course, possible that the Department had no such overall policy but simply proceeded on an ad hoc basis. That, however, would not leave the Department any less responsible for the unhappy circumstances that occurred.

If the policy adopted by the Department of Education seems lamentable, the conduct of the university presidents appears scarcely more distinguished by comparison. Several of their number seemed unaware of the significance or implications of the terms the government was proposing. Apparently they were prepared to commit their universities to agreements that gave the Department primary control in determining the pattern and nature of their teacher education program. It must be acknowledged that the universities were at the disadvantage of only beginning to develop cooperative structures to deal with the government. Had it not been for the intervention of the faculty association, that disadvantage might have proved even more damaging.

OCUFA's concern, naturally, was primarily for the interests of its members whose salaries, academic rank, and tenure were affected, in principle at least, by the conditions the Department proposed. At the same time, OCUFA was sensitive to the implications of the Department's policy in terms of the freedom of action of the universities to take a fresh approach to teacher education. It is not necessary to accept what might be regarded as OCUFA's traditional academic elitist bias on the subject in order to give that organization credit for recognizing the very real threat to reasonable university autonomy contained in the Department's amalgamation policy. On the difficult question of staffing, for example, OCUFA members might oppose the notion that a different set of paper and experience qualifications than the usual academic degrees was appropriate for faculty of education staff. Again, the Department's attempt to achieve full and automatic staff transfer to university rank was not conducive to a reasonable consideration of the issues involved. While no one would deny the necessity of protecting the security and interests of the staff of the teachers' colleges, the Department's policy seemed designed either to make them unwelcome members of the university community or to leave them entirely outside it.

It may be that the above assessment suffers from the fragmentary nature of the information now available or the misinterpretation of that evidence. If so, then the judgments regarding the relative burdens of responsibility will have to be revised in the future. One must certainly acknowledge that the tasks of transferring responsibility for teacher education from the Department to the universities and of developing diverse and improved programs were extremely difficult and complicated. Even with the most far-sighted and skillful policy on the part of the government and the most cordial and energetic cooperation of all the parties involved, the job would not have been easy. As it was, it seems safe to say that the government's efforts to reorganize and reform teacher education — announced in 1966 and suspended in 1971 — will remain, if not the major failure of the Davis era in Ontario education, at least the major disappointment.

NOTES

1. *Globe and Mail*, Toronto, August 20, 1971.
2. In 1966, the great bulk of Ontario's elementary school teachers were trained at thirteen teachers' colleges — Toronto, Lakeshore (also in Toronto), Hamilton, St. Catharines, London, Stratford, Windsor, Peterborough, Ottawa (one English- and one French-speaking), North Bay, Sudbury, and Lakehead — run by the Teacher Education Branch of the Department of Education. Most of the students at these institutions came directly from high school and did not have a university degree. All prospective secondary school teachers, on the other hand, were required to have an undergraduate degree and were trained in colleges of education attached to a university and jointly supervised by it and the government. In 1966, there were three of these colleges: at the University of Toronto; at Queen's University, Kingston; and at the University of Western Ontario, London.
3. Ontario, Legislative Assembly, *Debates*, 27th Leg., 4th Session, March 29, 1966, p. 2010.
4. Ibid., 5th Session, May 25, 1967, p. 3845; p. 3851.
5. Lakehead University, Thunder Bay, 1969; the University of Ottawa, 1969; the University of Windsor, 1970; Brock University, St. Catharines, 1971; and York University, Toronto, 1971.
6. *Report of the Minister's Committee on the Training of Elementary School Teachers, 1966* (Toronto: Ontario Department of Education, 1966). The chairman of the twenty-one-member committee was C. R. MacLeod, Superintendent of Public Schools and Assistant Director of Education, Windsor. This report is referred to hereafter as the MacLeod Report.
7. W. G. Fleming, *Ontario's Educative Society* (Toronto: University of Toronto Press, 1971), vol. 4, p. 1.
8. The MacLeod Report, p. 21.
9. Ibid., p. 34.
10. *Debates*, March 29, 1966, p. 2009.
11. Ibid., May 25, 1967, p. 3843. The three were Lakehead, Brock, and Laurentian universities.
12. Ibid., p. 3848; p. 3850.

13. Commission on Post-Secondary Education in Ontario, *Draft Report*, Douglas Wright, chairman (Toronto: Queen's Printer, 1971).

14. Fleming's account of these difficulties in *Ontario's Educative Society*, vol. 5, chap. 5, pp. 79–104, is excellent. The quotations in this paragraph are from p. 80 and p. 84. Fleming also notes that from then on, the university's board of governors did not bother to "approve" new appointments to the staff of the college; it merely "noted" that they had been made.

15. Ibid., p. 88.

16. Fleming gives a very fair-minded account in his book of the gradual relaxation of central control over the teachers' colleges and of their efforts to diversify their programs (vol. 5, pp. 24–42). The tradition of hierarchical authority, however, is not easily shaken off, and evidence of the inhibiting influence of the civil service mentality has remained.

17. It is worth noting that another government committee set up some years previously to examine the training of secondary school teachers in Ontario had rejected all other plans *but* the consecutive. *Report of the Minister's Committee on the Training of Secondary School Teachers, 1962* (Toronto: Ontario Department of Education, 1962), recommendation 3, p. 210.

18. The MacLeod Report, p. 24.

19. *Debates*, May 25, 1967, p. 3842.

20. For a university viewpoint, see the Ontario Confederation of University Faculty Associations (OCUFA), "A Policy Statement on the Amalgamation of Elementary Teachers' Colleges with the Universities," November 1968, pp. 9–10.

21. The MacLeod Report, p. 43.

22. Ibid., p. 22; p. 44.

23. *Debates*, May 25, 1967, p. 3842.

24. Quoted in OCUFA, "A Policy Statement," pp. 2–3.

25. OCUFA, ibid., pp. 14–15.

26. The driving force behind the York proposal and the subsequent efforts by that university to develop a teacher education program was John T. Saywell, Dean of Arts from 1964 to 1973. Without his strong leadership it is unlikely that York would have persevered in its negotiations with the Department. A notable feature of York's development of a teacher education program was the degree to which it invited outside scrutiny and criticism of its plans. As a result, the program that was finally initiated in 1972, while retaining the basic principles embodied in the 1965 proposal, was considerably modified in several important aspects. The York program is certainly the most substantially different development in Ontario teacher education to emerge during the reorganization process.

27. York University, *Senate Minutes*, "Report of the Interim Committee on the Planning and Implementation of a Faculty of Education at York University to the Senate Academic Policy and Planning Committee," 1971.

28. Committee of Presidents of Universities of Ontario (CPUO), *Collective*

Autonomy: Second Annual Review, 1967/68 (Toronto: University of Toronto Press, 1968), p. 21.

29. For a résumé of the Committee of Presidents' position, see CPUO, *Collective Autonomy*, pp. 22–23.

30. Ibid., p. 23.

31. See "Minutes of the Council of Deans of Arts and Science at the Ontario Universities, Fall Meeting, November 20/21, 1967," p. 5.

32. CPUO, "Principles and Guildelines/Augmented Statement," July 17, 1968. Quoted in David Saul, "The Story Behind the Amalgamation Delay" (unpublished research paper, Ontario Institute for Studies in Education, 1970), pp. 34, 35.

33. Quoted in Saul, "Amalgamation Delay," p. 44.

34. The following quotations from the "Memorandum of Understanding between the Deputy Minister of Education and Representatives of the Committee of Presidents Regarding the Proposed Integration of Teachers' Colleges into Universities, March 14, 1969" illustrate this point: the "Department of Education recognizes and accepts the autonomy of the universities and their inherent right . . . to establish and approve the curriculum of any program, subject only to the Minister's right of certification" (p. 1); the Advisory Committee "will in no way supplant the authority of the senate or board of the university" (p. 3); though the initial appointment of the head of teacher education would be made in consultation with the Department, that person "may or may not be the principal of the teachers' college being integrated" (p. 4); the rank of other staff members would be "at the discretion of the university," and they might be designated as "special lecturer or other appropriate category" (p. 4).

35. "Memorandum of Understanding," pp. 4–5. OCUFA regarded this "screening-out" process to be much more difficult than an initial "screening-in" process and, at one point in the negotiations, described it as doing the Department's "dirty work." In either case, it should be noted, the staff of the teachers' colleges were left in a very uncomfortable position. In practice, the staff of the teachers' colleges that were amalgamated after 1969 seem to have been treated fairly. Almost all were granted academic rank at the assistant professor level. Procedures were established for reviewing their status; and where this review has occurred so far, almost all have been granted tenure. At York University, the pattern has been quite different. There, the teachers' college, while officially part of the university, has continued to function separately while a faculty of education is being established. The masters have not been granted academic rank, and it is not yet clear how their long-term status and employment will be dealt with.

36. CPUO, *Campus and Forum: Third Annual Review, 1968–69* (Toronto: University of Toronto Press, 1969), pp. 20–21.

Avoiding Guaranteed Failure

Verner Smitheram and Eric S. Hillis

Predicting failure in any given area of human endeavor is relatively easy. In teacher education, it is ridiculously easy. The pitfalls are so well known that stumbling into them seems inexcusable. Yet there is a danger that this will happen as teachers' colleges become amalgamated with the universities of Ontario. Concern for the immediate political issues of amalgamation in combination with existing constraints may obscure the primary need to set program objectives and create a program design. If these two aspects of teacher education cannot be decided well ahead of amalgamation deadlines, hurried programming may result, and some universities may instinctively reach for certain obvious answers to programming that require minimal changes in present university policies. The danger is real since few universities relish the prospect of association with teacher education.

Often a great deal of controversy is sparked both inside and outside the university when universities first offer teacher education programs. To ensure that such controversy is kept to a minimum and that existing programs are affected as little as possible, the university need only ensure —

1. that the teacher education component is kept at low status and isolated from academic faculties;
2. that all former "masters" and future instructors of teachers become subject specialists;
3. that the institutional roles remain ambiguous;
4. that explicit program objectives are judiciously avoided;
5. that the program structures are as rigid as possible;
6. that the typical academic/professional, theory/practice, pre-service/in-service gaps are reinforced;

7. that field experience is restricted to short intermittent periods or relegated to an internship following formal academic and professional studies;
8. that only consecutive programs are allowed;
9. that responsibility for educational decision making is accepted only when it cannot be avoided.

Implementation of the above policies will not only successfully deaden the pains of amalgamation, it will also *guarantee the failure of teacher education*. Although (whatever policies are pursued) success cannot be guaranteed, clearly policies such as these must be avoided or offset if even a potential for success is to exist. The following discussion offers some workable alternatives that reduce the probability of inherently futile programs.

Problems of Amalgamation and Integration

The first problem to be resolved is the mechanics of institutional amalgamation. Many promising programs and courses will never leave the planning stage unless they can operate in a context that is sympathetic to the demands of professional training.

Various structures are possible — departments, faculties, colleges, schools — but these should not be viewed as a continuum ranging from the least to the most desirable. Choice of a particular structure should be based upon the most effective balance that can be achieved between autonomy and mutual cooperation. No given structure guarantees this, but some structures offer a less hostile environment than do others.

The introduction of a teacher education program into a university introduces variables not present in other disciplines. First, the program is staffed by persons whose qualifications are heavily weighted in favor of practical experience and whose salaries have a readily identifiable market level. Budgets must reflect this, and they must also allow for equipment and supply needs that differ greatly from those of traditional humanities departments.

Second, the program itself is designed to achieve a more specific objective than that of most other undergraduate programs. Its students are being prepared for a particular position in a specific area and must be judged on criteria beyond their purely academic performance. Particularly contentious problems will arise if students are asked to leave a program merely for academic reasons.

Autonomy should not be granted at the expense of total separation of the teacher education component from the rest of the university community, for this may perpetuate the ghetto-like isolation that unhappily surrounds professional teacher preparation at many universities. Although there are attractions in a closed program where all the students intend to be public school teachers, and where all their professors have been ones, the advantages of this system are largely overshadowed by the narrowness of the experience.

On balance, given the differing demands of an education program and the need for a close working relationship with the rest of the university, we feel that the establishment of a faculty of education is the most desirable approach. This structure allows for initial control over budgeting, hiring, and programming, while retaining the highest potential for development in a total university context.

A second problem is the merging of the faculty of a teachers' college with the university faculty. Complex prejudices surround this issue, but essentially the difficulty is that persons who are qualified to teach within an education program often do not meet the traditional criteria for the hiring of university faculty. It should not be assumed that the university faculty can take over all the duties originally assigned to the teachers' colleges, any more than that teachers' colleges can take over the duties of the university. Any joining of staff must recognize the unique professional contribution made by the colleges and, as a possible compromise, offer generous sabbaticals to allow satisfaction of university requirements — whether these meet real or imagined needs.

The problem of providing good instruction will not be resolved merely by upgrading the academic qualifications of teaching faculty. This is especially true where the instruction of student teachers is concerned. In granting faculty status to teachers in education, there must be acceptance of the principle that a variety of experiences and non-academic qualifications are at least as important as traditional educational qualifications.

Few, if any, provinces have adequately defined the role that they expect teacher education programs and institutions to play. Indeed, most programs develop rather haphazardly, on the basis of such fluctuating considerations as the varying competencies of the staff from year to year. Programs that evolve in this way make very efficient use of faculty, but there is little evidence that such courses are "relevant" to students' needs. This situation results from the failure to set up any machinery to evaluate the changing needs of school systems. Programs should never be regarded as having achieved a final, fixed form. The proof of this lies in the fact that faculty often are faced with a basic conflict between their responsibility to service a school system and their desire to do what they personally feel is best for it.

Obvious problems arise if an institution pursues only its own lights. There is little advantage in turning out a quantity of prospective teachers with a particular skill if the hiring board does not consider the skill necessary or even desirable. At the same time, institutions that produce teachers who can only serve a static system do little to fulfill their role as "agents of change." In a large province, there must be room for programs at both ends of the scale and a variety of shades in between. But the role of the institution must be predetermined to some extent if any rational pattern is to emerge.

Another area of confusion arises concerning the population the institution is meant to serve. Comments often are made implying a lack of maturity on the part of students — for example, "We find teachers who return to take a professional program are more capable students." Rather than being criticisms of individual students, such views reflect a basic failure to distinguish between pre-service and in-service programming. At the very least, institutions should broadly state the kinds of activities that are best carried on prior to actual teaching experience and the kinds of programs that are enhanced by previous teaching experience. Some of the most bitter criticisms of teacher education programs come from individuals with in-service needs who take courses with pre-service aims, and vice versa.

Finally, some attempt must be made to predict the future needs of our education system. Although throughout the past decade there have been discussions concerning an impending oversupply of teachers, no long-range planning has resulted. Now, with the fact upon us, decisions with far-reaching implications are being made on an ad hoc basis. Such crisis planning is not an adequate foundation for program design. At a time when education costs are under critical public scrutiny, it is willful waste to prepare more teachers than are actually needed.

These considerations lead us to some observations about the general atmosphere in which Ontario teacher education is being reorganized. The expressed attitudes of most administrative officials involved in the proposed amalgamations are overwhelmingly colored by a sense of restriction, a lack of freedom, and a frustrated acceptance of carefully prescribed boundaries. To the detached observer, the word that seems to sum up most discussions is *constraint*.

Many innovative ideas are set aside in the face of objections that some rule or certification regulation or related educational agency (such as a board, a teachers' federation, the Ministry of Education, or a university senate) will not allow such and such to happen. For example, experienced teachers who do not meet University of Toronto graduate regulations are barred from graduate degree programs at the Ontario Institute for Studies in Education. They are not admitted to such programs, even though they have proven abilities that would make them worthwhile contributors. Concurrent programs are feared because of a reluctance on the part of some university senates to create new B.Ed. degrees. The entry of psychology, sociology, and philosophy majors into the school system is restricted by certification regulations. Programs that do not conform to specific numbers and kinds of academic and professional credits demanded by certification regulations must be rejected.

These and many other examples reflect the fact that structural considerations in the Ontario education system have been and still are viewed in a narrow prescriptive fashion. In effect, they are used as organizational straitjackets, having as their primary function the prohibition of a host of possibilities and the endorsement of very few. This has resulted in limited conceptualization of teacher education, resistance to innovations that do not conform to present structures, and frustration of students and student teachers. In the schools, where needed competencies change while regulations for teacher education do not, there occurs a rejection of what is taught in teacher preparation institutions and acquiescence in "the way things have always been done."

In a changing educational context, rigid structures must be rejected in favor of flexible structures that facilitate rather than hamper responses to needed changes. Specifically, structures should be designed (*a*) to create an atmosphere congenial to change, (*b*) to break down barriers between education agencies, and (*c*) to enhance the interrelation of components of teacher education programs.

The limitations of structures must be kept in mind. First, although structures can facilitate certain kinds of outcomes, they do not in themselves guarantee their achievement. Second, if they are too detailed and too dogmatically developed, structures can take on a life of their own; and when they do so, form takes precedence over function. That this often occurs is very much in evidence in most of our institutions. It should always be remembered that structures are instrumental means to the performance of certain functions. Third, structures can fail if they are spun off spasmodically in reaction to isolated problems. They need to be oriented to a focal point that will give them purpose. In this case, the focal point should be some conception of the kind of teacher desired. Fourth, structures can be impediments to progress if they are arbitrarily imposed from above, because they may be inappropriate or, worse, they may generate concerted resistance on the part of those who have to implement such edicts. The Ontario government runs the risk of carrying on most of the present discussions and negotiations in an atmosphere of almost open hostility. The decision-making process, however, must involve all the people affected by those decisions. In the Ontario situation, the best-designed program will founder and the best motive become base if it is imposed, regardless of how benevolently.

Total Program Objectives

The internal structures of programs cannot be designed in abstraction from a conception of the objectives of a program. Structures are instrumental means to an end. Since the end of any teacher education program is the development of effective teachers for the schools of today and tomorrow, structural considerations must be guided to a large extent by a logically determined concept of the teacher desired.

The guiding concept of the teacher may be formulated from many different points of view. Some will prefer to define the teacher in broad philosophical terms; others, in more specific functional terms. It is our belief that a thorough approach will require a philosophical ground, but it must be one that can be translated into more precise functional terms issuing from a task analysis. In other words, program development must be based on expectations about what we want teachers to do, while making clear the philosophical rationale about why we want them to perform certain tasks. Once it is known which tasks may be justified as desirable, some useful inferences can be made about the kind of education teachers should receive. When these inferences are organized in a coherent fashion, there results a concept of the teacher that may serve as a useful model for teacher preparation.

The trouble with most discussions of the concept of the teacher is that perspectives on the matter are highly varied. As a result, differences rather than similarities are stressed until the possibility of agreement disappears. This is not to suggest that it is impossible to formulate a relatively clear-cut concept. Rather the difficulty lies in a tendency to strive for a single conception of the teacher that encompasses all the myriad objectives that can be set for the ideal teacher. The result is usually an impasse, or a conception that is all but impossible to realize because it demands an omnicapable teacher. In all other fields, it is understood that no single person can display the entire range of skills and abilities required for the field as a whole. Musicians rarely attempt to become expert in playing all the instruments of an orchestra. Teachers, then, should not be expected to play all the possible roles involved in the teaching–learning process; instead, they should be selective and play a few roles effectively. It must be frankly acknowledged that no single institution can develop teachers able to meet all the needs of all the schools and of all the pupils in the province.

In a province like Ontario, which has a multiplicity of teacher preparation institutions, each institution must seek its own distinctive approach. By adopting a more modest and specific approach to the setting of objectives, much can be done to increase the likelihood of reaching agreement on the concept of the teacher that is to prevail at each institution. This strategy will require cooperation at the provincial level, both to avoid needless duplication and to ensure that the entire spectrum of needs in Ontario schools will be served by the aggregate of teacher education institutions.

To decide which of the distinct conceptions shall prevail at any given institution and to select the range of conceptions required to serve the needs of the entire province, two things need to be done. In the first place, it must be decided which teacher types are desired. The responsibility for initiating this decision should to a significant degree be shouldered by teachers and principals, who are most knowledgeable about the needs of pupils in schools. Second, it must be decided what means are to be used to develop teachers who will be able to meet these needs. Teacher educators in faculties of education must assume the major responsibility for this set of choices.

Research of the second kind depends upon the success of the first and involves an analysis of what counts as effective teaching. Even cursory acquaintance with the literature makes it clear that research has not produced a universally acceptable criterion of teaching effectiveness. Most of the studies — and they number in the thousands — are based on empirical and statistical methods using questionnaires, inventories, ratings, tests, and so on. Clearly it is not for lack of effort that real progress has eluded researchers.

One explanation of this phenomenon is that

> any study of ability depends upon a conception of what constitutes successful functioning. Before definitive research on the factors associated with effectiveness can be pursued, it must be possible to specify some criterion through which effectiveness may be identified. Research based upon a clearly unacceptable criterion cannot produce results of any great significance.[1]

We further suggest that the criterion of success is a matter of decision. Effectiveness is not inherent in teaching itself, but is a relational quality — that is, teaching act X is effective/ineffective insofar as it produces some specified desirable/undesirable outcome. The point, then, is that teaching, to be judged successful, must be viewed in terms of goals, and the goals are a matter of value judgment, not fact finding.

This does not remove the difficulty of achieving consensus about the goals to be pursued, but it does discourage futile attempts to think of teaching in isolation from the goals of education. Much of the mystique about what constitutes "good" teaching would disappear if goals were made explicit, because it is in terms of the latter that the former is to be judged. Those who recoil at the difficulty of explicitly stating their goals should bear in mind that decisions about goals are made constantly, but that to avoid overt disagreements, they usually remain implicit. A certain uneasy peace among educators is maintained at the price of random educational drifting.

In a survey of United States teacher training colleges, it was found that many programs failed because there was an inadequate conceptualization of the *total* program. If the assumptions upon which a program is built remain implicit rather than explicit, it is very difficult to select rationally the skills, attitudes, methods, and knowledge that an effective teacher is likely to need. Since the range of options is clearly too immense for any one program to inculcate, selection is necessary. If that is the case, arbitrariness can be avoided only if selection is made from a point of view. The choice of a point of view must be based on a synthesis of research about the needs of the community in which the teacher is to serve, and on research and theory concerning the development of effective teachers.

Although having a point of view is necessary, it is not sufficient in itself. Many programs based on an explicit concept of the teacher's role have failed because of an inability to specify their goals in terms that are precise enough to permit direct inferences about the action to be taken. If the stated goals are vague and general, they provide little direction for program design.

It should also be stressed that evaluation of programs is possible only on the basis of some definition of goals. Up to the present, programs have rarely been evaluated, for want of criteria by which to judge them. This accounts in part for the astonishing ossification of most teacher preparation curricula.[2] In a world of change, goals as well as the means taken to achieve them must undergo constant reality testing.

Articulation of a total program perspective would do much to destroy the faint-hearted approach of so-called reformers of teacher education who equate change with tinkering. In the absence of a resolve to alter the fundamental basis of present ineffective programs, innovations will continue to be of the timid, piecemeal kind that have characterized most developments in teacher education. In a program aimed at producing teachers who are almost exclusively subject-centered information transmitters, no purpose is served by introducing a few weeks of instruction in how the teacher can function as a student-centered resource person. The two approaches are so different that the innovations cannot be understood in their own terms. Examples of this minimizing of innovations through absorption within traditional conceptions are readily available. For instance, teachers trained as information givers tend to view videotape simply as a tool for doing on a more massive scale exactly what was done in the past — transmitting a talking face. In this case, an actual regression is perceived, because the audience is not present to provide the feedback that is available in a face-to-face meeting.

Clarity in program perspectives will enable those in charge of programs to develop a realistic staffing policy. If a faculty of education selects a certain model for teacher training, it can then seek to attract a compatible staff. In this way, the various instruction components of the program may reinforce one another. Where the faculty members do not have any objectives in common, the resulting eclecticism leaves students in a greater state of confusion than is necessary or good for them. The point is not that it is desirable to achieve a bland uniformity within a given faculty of education, but that there should be a few basic, common links if a program is to develop as an integrated whole.

If total program perspectives are articulated by each of the different faculties of education in the province and are widely publicized, the prospective student teacher will have the advantage of being able to choose a course of training that is suitable for him. Furthermore, if the programs are successful and do produce distinguishable types of graduates, school systems also may select their personnel with the knowledge that, if they come from a certain institution, they will in all probability have certain orientations to education as well as specific capabilities.

Fundamental Problems in Concurrent Teacher Education Programs
Generally speaking, pedagogues recognize two types of programs: the concurrent and the consecutive.

The concurrent program presents both professional courses and academic courses over the period of study for an undergraduate degree. It does not seem to have enjoyed much popularity in Ontario — partly, one suspects, because of a belief that academic courses are in some way contaminated by the mingling. The arguments, like those against miscegenation, are primarily emotional. Concurrent programming does, however, offer specific advantages:

> The concurrent program [is] the most desirable for the preparation of teachers. The student has the time to be introduced gradually to the schools and to acquire some confidence in the school situation. The student is not faced with the rather sudden pressures attendant upon entering a program one September, with the knowledge that he has to face a class the following September. This provision for reflective thought about the profession is essential, and only the concurrent program presently provides the time.[3]

The consecutive program is likely to result if education staff and students are isolated. This type of program is traditionally embedded in Canadian education, providing a means of converting a liberal arts education into professional teacher preparation by the addition of roughly one year of further study. This is the rationale behind the one-year B.Ed. course following an undergraduate degree.

It is argued that the attraction of the consecutive program, other than its speed and its separation from academic study, is that it enables student teachers to take all their courses in the education faculty so they can engage in practice teaching without interrupting their academic course work. This is the only way that they can have any long exposure in the schools if the university does not operate on a semester system. Also, the program provides for the entry of latecomers to the profession.

This last argument is not supportable. Apart from the fact that no other profession feels the need to accommodate latecomers in this way, if teaching is as complex and children are as sensitive as research leads us to believe, it is absurd to assume that teachers can be adequately trained for their profession over such a short period. Not only is it absurd; it is unfair to both the school system and the pupils to maintain that such graduates can function with any high degree of competence in their first years.

In addition, the rationale underlying the introduction of consecutive programming in Ontario is no longer valid. While the province was experiencing a shortage of qualified teachers, some scheme was needed for quickly converting any college graduate into a teacher, and this system served its purpose well. But conditions have changed, so that today the program is an anachronism.

On balance, we cannot find any justification for the continued offering of consecutive programs. Thus, our discussion in this section is presented strictly within the context of the concurrent program. As we will demonstrate, the benefits of education courses are most easily realized in a four or five-year program of this type.

The Academic/Professional Gap

The atmosphere of mutual distrust and suspicion that often characterizes relations between academics in faculties of arts and sciences and their colleagues in faculties of education is far from inevitable, provided that each side remains sensitive to the problems of the other. The academic's dislike of teacher education is probably based on a virtually exclusive conception of the teacher as scholar. Many refuse to distinguish between knowing something and knowing how to teach it, and they believe that the obvious remedy for teacher incompetence is to prescribe even greater doses of subject knowledge. The logical limit (absurdity) of this argument is presumably that if every teacher had a Ph.D., the schools would flourish.

While it is true, of course, that subject knowledge is the *sine qua non* of good teaching, it must be recognized that there are great dimensions of the teaching act that require skills scholarship does not provide. Moreover, recent studies have made it clear that the university, the traditional home of the scholar, is plagued by bad teaching practices.[4] Indeed, as university personnel should realize, most of the attacks upon teacher education programs are, with slight alterations, equally applicable to present university programs. It can be asked of both areas: does tradition override actual needs? Is the teaching effective? Are the best means of instruction utilized? Are programs client-centered? These questions and others pertain to universities as well as to teachers' colleges. At the level of teaching effectiveness, it would be difficult to make a case for the superiority of either institution.

The university academic must come to understand this if he is to be at all sympathetic to a faculty of education. But more than this, he must admit that he has a large responsibility for the success of teacher education. Soon all teachers will be expected to hold a university degree and to acquire a sound liberal arts or science background.[5] That aspect of teaching which demands scholarship is largely in the hands of the academic departments. The maximization of the benefits of general education for the teacher will not be achieved, however, if academic departments limit their interest solely to teaching subject matter. They can also contribute directly to improving teaching competence on the part of student teachers by conveying knowledge about knowledge. Would it not, for example, be a great asset for future teachers to be able to identify the forms of knowledge involved in their teaching subjects? This point was clearly made in *Teachers for the Real World*:

> The subject matter of each field of teaching is a mixture of different forms of knowledge. All of the fields contain concepts. Some contain laws or law-like statements, others contain rules and theorems. And still others include values either as major emphases or as incidental to other forms of content. It is important for the teacher to be aware of these knowledge forms because studies have shown that each is taught and learned in a different way. Current programs of subject matter preparation do not enable a teacher to identify the forms of subject matter or to relate teaching behavior appropriately to the ways they are most easily learned.[6]

Attention to this often overlooked aspect of subject teaching would benefit the professor as well as the student teacher.

Arts and science departments can exert further influence on the caliber of graduate teachers by designating members who will make some special effort to become knowledgeable about school problems in their subject areas. Some of the possibilities in this regard are cited in the

AVOIDING GUARANTEED FAILURE 63

University of Prince Edward Island report *Teacher Education: Perseverance or Professionalism*. One of the recommendations encourages

> each university department teaching subjects included in the school curriculum to
> (*a*) seek improved communication with school teachers in the corresponding subject area,
> (*b*) seek representation on school curriculum committees,
> (*c*) distribute to the school principals, a list of faculty along with their special competencies and interests,
> (*d*) organize *ad hoc* workshops to be presented to school teachers upon request,
> (*e*) offer in co-operation with the Extension Department, credit and non-credit courses [for teachers] in diverse localities of the province,
> (*f*) provide, as a diagnostic service, information about the strengths and deficiencies of students . . . entering the University.[7]

The report further recommends the establishment of associations of school and university teachers to coordinate the above activities and to form subgroupings of teachers and faculty in each subject area. This kind of university involvement with the schools and with practicing teachers would doubtless offer a much sounder basis for the provision of effective assistance to the student teachers presently attending university.

It is hoped that if members of faculties of arts and science establish some rapport with members of faculties of education, involve themselves with schools and teachers, and make special efforts to examine and teach particular forms of knowledge in diverse subject areas, the principle of university-wide responsibility for teacher education may become meaningful.

The Theory/Practice Gap

> Teachers must be prepared in such a way that teaching does not devolve into a simple mechanical process, nor, at the other extreme, must teaching be a purely subjective art devoid of any ground rules.[8]

No attempts will be made here to analyze or justify the role of theory. Rather, for our purposes, it is assumed that educational theory is necessary, and that it will and should continue to constitute a major portion of teacher education programs.

It is accepted that the relationship between general theoretical statements and practical action statements has not been adequately explained by philosophers or scientists. It is also clear that unless all theories are to be judged sterile, a connection must be admitted between theory and practice. The issue, then, is not whether theory is relevant to practice, but *how* it is relevant. To short-circuit the last point, as seems appropriate in the context of this paper, we will assume that there is a high probability that the best results in any given activity are achieved by those who can theorize about that activity as well as perform it.

If this assumption is correct, the dictum that "practice without theory is blind, and theory without practice is useless" must be taken seriously as a major consideration in the design of program structures.

The problem can be expressed in this way: how can structures facilitate the necessary reciprocation between theory and practice? More specifically, how can the primarily theoretical components of programs (general education, curriculum and instruction, educational foundations) be fruitfully interrelated to the primarily practical components of programs (field experience, methodology, professional studies)?

Just as no theory has ever been devised without prior apprehension of a question, so no theory is ever truly learned unless the learner can apprehend the question for which the theory is a response. Too often theory is taught as a set of answers looking for questions; certainly this is the case when student teachers are asked to undertake all kinds of courses in educational theory before they have had any experience as teachers in schools.

It seems eminently sensible to expose prospective teachers to a significant experience core early in their studies. We would go further and urge that all the professional components of programs be organized around a core of field experience — that is, insofar as it is possible and realistic, the order, sequence, and content of all components should be decided with reference to the experience core.

The experience core must be designed to provide a basically realistic exposure to the classroom, allowing student teachers to participate fully in the life of the school and experience all its problems. Ideally this should consist of at least two one-semester periods of immersion in the schools, with one or more intervening semesters at the university.

If the university is not on the semester system, a year-long experience core in the penultimate year (at the latest) may be made available, though this is less satisfactory. It is imperative that the school experience be broken up by a period in the university prior to full-time employment in a school, so that students may have an opportunity to view their university studies in the perspective of real school problems. Alternatively, student teachers may withdraw from academic courses for a year of professional studies and field experience. The McGill University Elementary Education Teaching-Teams program (MEET) provides a useful model: students are required to spend three days a week in schools and two days at university.

Obviously, raw experience alone is not sufficient. To maximize the benefits, the following considerations must be taken into account:
1. The field experience must be preceded by a period of simple observation by the student with the intent of affording an opportunity for him to select the school, the grade level, and the supervising teacher best suited to him.
2. An orientation program must be developed that provides the basic information required to ease him into the school setting.
3. A graduated series of experiences must be provided, ranging from observation to full responsibility for a class.
4. Opportunities for reflection upon the experience must be provided while the experience is occurring. This implies adequate supervision by members of the faculty of education and counseling by supervising teachers within the schools, as well as peer companionship and criticism.
5. Peer criticism can be built into the program by the use of teams of student teachers at the initial stages of the field experience. If the supervising teachers are to provide worthwhile guidance and evaluation, they must be fully acquainted with the program and its objectives, and they must also have sound knowledge about the students under their direction.
6. The field experience must be designed to counter the tendency to acquiesce in the way things have always been done in the schools.
7. The program must be designed so that it is an asset to the school system as well as a training opportunity for the student.
8. The remainder of the professional program must be planned in such a way that it exploits, complements, and extends the benefits of the experience core.

Any program that exploits the field experience in these ways solves many of the problems encountered in contemporary teacher preparation. These considerations should not be construed, however, as advocacy of a strictly skill- and technique-oriented approach to teaching. Just as teaching behavior cannot be based solely on learning theory and philosophical derivation, neither can it be based solely on techniques and skills. There is a complementarity here that structures must reflect.

The program must allow for individualized study, so that problems that arise during the field experience can be pursued at the university in a more formal manner. In this way, new approaches can be developed and then tested in a realistic school setting. This experience also can be used as a basis for self-evaluation (How well — or badly — am I doing? Why? How might I improve?) and for self-analysis (What kind of teacher am I? Why do I want to be a teacher? What values am I promoting?). Providing time for this sort of reflective thinking can build a self-screening mechanism into the program, giving the student the opportunity consciously to choose his career rather than follow the line of least resistance.

One of the most attractive benefits of such an approach in a concurrent program is the fact that once students have successfully completed the first in-school experience, they are much more confident about their survival in the system. It is fair to say that lack of such confidence characterizes most programs of short duration and makes it impossible for students to reflect upon the problems that teaching may present. With more time for analysis and evaluation, the students can examine what actually does go on in school, instead of finding themselves in the "recognize it, remember it, and copy it" framework.

If the experience in the internship can become the basis for a critical frame of reference about traditional procedures, and can produce a frame of mind that reconciles the possible with the desirable, much will have been done to ensure innovative approaches. It cannot be emphasized too strongly that we feel that educational change will not result from the acquisition of nuts-and-bolts skills; rather, it will result from the way individuals view their role, including the application of these skills.

Carefully designed experience cores also will bring about benefits outside the reference of the particular program. The field experience is almost the only area of contact among the various agencies involved in education, and more often than not, it has been an area of conflict. Successful organization of the experience core will encourage cooperation among universities, school boards, and teachers, and this cooperation can have many other beneficial side effects.

The Pre-Service/In-Service Gap

The confusion surrounding the role of programs and program components was alluded to earlier. Clarification is needed in the minds of both teachers and universities as to what constitutes relevant pre-service education as opposed to in-service programming. The basic problem may indeed lie in the fact that this distinction is made at all, for it implies that the two periods can be completely separated. The value of a program organized around an experience core is that such a distinction blurs when the theoretical and the practical overlap.

The facts remain, however, that some courses are taught from one perspective or the other and that students tend to take these courses for one of two purposes: to prepare them to face a classroom, or to enable them to cope with problems they have encountered in the classroom. If there is a variance between the perspective offered by the instructor and the purpose seen by the student, little will emerge in the way of useful educational experience.

The worst conflicts arise because minimum standards for qualified teachers are constantly changing. As a result, experienced teachers who have not completed what are presently considered to be the entrance requirements for new teachers (a B.A., B.Ed., or similar degree) often return to full-time study. While the desire of these individuals to return to study is laudable, their treatment by the universities is not. The almost automatic response on the part of the institution is to steer them into the program designed for preparing new teachers. This is neither relevant to their needs, nor applicable to their experience.

This difficulty is one of our own making. No other profession subjects experienced practitioners to preparatory training programs. But then no other profession has allowed such minimally qualified persons to practice. Given the situation, we cannot apologetically dismiss the criticisms of these teachers by saying the programs are not really meant for them. Different programs must be designed, and probably new insights can be gained about the preparatory programs that are at present required.

Rule by Default

Education in Canada, and teacher education in particular, is characterized by a failure to assume responsibility and a corresponding readiness to complain when decisions are made elsewhere. The operational doctrine seems to be to make sure that the buck doesn't stop here. Agencies that should cooperate defend assumed territorial imperatives that are increasingly irrelevant to the massive educational system we have constructed. Ontario is probably no worse than any other province, but size makes the problem in this province more apparent. Any discussion of proposed changes brings forth pleadings of inability because of a constraint here or a regulation there, and so things proceed (or rather, remain at a standstill). Decisions are deferred until inaction becomes tradition and ad hoc arrangements become hard-and-fast rules.

A case in point might be the current discussions about the possibilities of screening applicants for education programs. While it is widely agreed that teachers should not be chosen solely on an academic basis, most institutions that do limit enrollment employ just that criterion. Attempts to find other approaches usually bring forth comments to the effect that it is not the job of the university to screen before enrollment. Others argue that failure to complete the program successfully is screening; beyond this, graduates take their chances in the marketplace. The government position is that if a prospective teacher has completed the prescribed course, he will receive a teaching license. The teachers' federation will accept him into membership if he has a job.

The only body that makes a real decision is the hiring board. While universities and governments and teachers' organizations decry the possibilities of constructing any valid screening device, boards are being forced to do exactly this. By default, the responsibility has devolved to them, and they receive little assistance from any other agency.

If any real gains are to be made, the aura of competition must disappear. Public confidence is strained and undermined by the lack of cooperation and the squabbles that permeate much educational discussion. If we are to retain our credibility for an informed and increasingly critical taxpayer, we must assume the maturity and accept the responsibility that participation demands.

In the words of Walt Kelly's Pogo, "We have met the enemy and he is us."

NOTES

1. Ronald T. Hyman, *Contemporary Thought on Teaching* (Englewood Cliffs, N.J.: Prentice-Hall, 1971), p. 213.

2. Geraldine Channon, "Trends in Teacher Preparation Curricula in Canada" (paper presented at the annual meeting of the American Educational Research Association, New York, February 1971).

3. Committee on Teacher Education, *Teacher Education: Perseverance or Professionalism*, V. Smitheram, chairman (Charlottetown: University of Prince Edward Island, 1971), p. 41.

4. See, for example, *Undergraduate Instruction in Arts and Science: Report of the Presidential Advisory Committee on Undergraduate Instruction in the Faculty of Arts and Sciences, University of Toronto*, C. B. MacPherson, chairman (Toronto: University of Toronto Press, 1967).

5. In 1969, the Department (now Ministry) of Education announced that by September, 1973, all teachers in Ontario's public and separate schools would be required to hold a university degree from an accredited institution.

6. Smith et al., *Teachers for the Real World*, p. 127.

7. Committee on Teacher Education, *Teacher Education*, p. 105.

8. Ibid., p. 46.

Continuing Education: A Neglected Concept

Robert Gidney, Philip Linden, and Geoffrey Milburn

The task of satisfactorily defining the term *professional* has frustrated many writers, but it is generally asserted that professionals possess certain identifiable skills and knowledge that can be subjected to external examination. Moreover, such persons seem also to strive for and demonstrate the regular reassessment and renewal of their competency. Old skills are often outdated skills, knowledge learned in initial training courses is frequently obsolete knowledge, and the experience based on outdated skills and obsolete knowledge is sterile experience. Given the knowledge explosion, rapid changes within society, and shifts in value systems and needs, professional persons in the future will have to be more skilled, more flexible, and more knowledgeable as the years go by. They will not be able to rely for long on initial training experiences. How, then, can we encourage professionals to change, to adapt, to contribute in new ways to differing situations — in a word, to *renew* their competence?

To ask this question of the teaching profession at the present time is both appropriate and timely. The supply crisis is now over, the basic education qualification of a bachelor's degree has been established in Ontario, and the profession as a whole seems more stable and better prepared than it has been in the past. We are entering a decade in which, if we so choose, we can design and implement new types of continuing education programs with unprecedented deliberation and forethought.

For the past ten years, we have been much more concerned with recruiting new teachers than with renewing the professional skills of those who are already qualified. The emphasis in the next decade should shift from initial training to continuing training, and from pre-service in in-service activities and programs. Few will regret the demise of the stopgap measures and patchwork policies that characterized teacher education in the late 1950s and early 1960s. The opportunity for a greatly increased concentration of provincial efforts upon continuing education should not be missed.

It is by no means certain, however, that such a commitment will be made. Indeed, there is sufficient evidence of differences of opinion and confusion in government circles, in boards of education and training institutions, and among teachers themselves to raise serious doubts that the significance of continuing education is clearly perceived or that a coherent policy is developing. The purpose of this article is to identify and examine the central issues in this area, to describe the present attitudes of the Ministry, boards, faculties, and teachers, and to explore some of the policy alternatives that emerge.

Issues and Alternatives

What do we mean by the phrase "the continuing education of teachers"? As a colleague has recently suggested, continuing education, like teaching itself, does not fit one particular mold but may take many forms.[1] We can broadly identify three training needs that are necessary in teaching, as in other professions. First, there is the need for what might be called (perhaps unkindly) "survival-kit updating" — the preparation of teachers for a new program of studies, a new subject area, or a new administrative post. Second, there is the need for refresher work in classroom practice. This includes expanding and deepening the teacher's knowledge of current developments in his subject and of curriculum theory and pedagogical techniques related to his subject. Third, there is the need for continuing education in areas of general professional concern — in matters of immediate interest and controversy, such as community involvement in the schools, and in long-term issues, such as the potential impact of new learning theory or technological innovation. These three activities generally encompass our expectations of teacher education. Some are simple and short term; others are complex and must develop over a long period of time. All of them, however, are related to the renewal of a teacher's expertise. Most of us would agree that they are desirable and necessary elements of teacher education.

Some may argue that Ontario teachers have been doing these things for years and that there is nothing new about our views on continuing education. But we believe that there has been a good deal of confusion between those activities designed to bring teachers' qualifications up to accepted minimum standards and those designed to renew the competence of qualified personnel. Massive support is given to the former, but only lip service is paid to the latter. This confusion over purpose has created traditions and channeled expectations in patterns that inhibit rather than enhance the professional growth of Ontario teachers. We maintain, in short, that much greater emphasis must be placed on programs of renewal, and there is substantial evidence to support our argument.

In the first place, the gap between rhetoric and reality in professional development is very wide. In theory, everyone acknowledges the importance of all three kinds of activities mentioned earlier; in practice, serious attention is given only to survival-kit updating. Despite the investment of time and effort in a very wide range of professional activities, only by the most generous overstatement can these programs be considered to contribute to professional *renewal*. In effect we have been patching up inadequacies rather than renewing previously learned skills.

This may appear to be a grossly unfair judgment. If one counts the number of courses taken by teachers each year over the last decade, the results are impressive. In 1969/70, for example, about 20,000 teachers enrolled in Ministry and local board certificate courses. An equal number took university undergraduate courses and high school specialist courses. A list of the number of workshops and short courses carried on in southwestern Ontario alone would fill several pages.

These enrollment figures must be interpreted with some care. Large numbers of teachers *do* take courses; but in most cases, these courses are designed to give teachers the *minimum* standard necessary to practice their profession. The B.A. has now become the minimum basic standard for elementary school teachers, and the specialist B.A. has long been the preferred basic standard for high school teachers. Many of the Ministry certificate courses are specifically designed to bring teachers up to an adequate level of competence in a new subject or a new curriculum. These courses do not contribute to the continuing education of professionals; rather, they reflect an attempt to ensure that teachers meet the minimum standards necessary to do their jobs. To put it another way, they represent that part of continuing education designed to complete pre-service training or to compensate for its deficiencies. We are not opposed to these activities, nor do we regard them as unnecessary or invalid — quite the contrary. But we do argue that the emphasis given to this type of work has drawn our attention away from important aspects of the professional growth of teachers.

In the second place, the commitment to survival courses has deeply affected the attitudes and policies of the Ministry, faculties of education, boards, and professional organizations. All seem committed to a type of continuing education that is designed to rectify immediate problems or inadequacies.

The attitude of the Ministry, for example, is best revealed in the kind of courses it offers and the kind of certification it will approve. In 1969/70, about 14,000 teachers took Ministry summer courses. Of these, 10,000 were concentrated in the following areas: art, elementary education, library, guidance, special education, teaching the trainable retarded, French, physical education, primary methods, and courses for elementary and secondary school principals. There was virtually no provision for any updating or refresher courses in high school subjects and only very limited provision for the core academic subjects in elementary school. The Ministry may believe that these needs are being met in other ways, but clearly it does not feel responsible for professional development beyond basic certification.

Recent publications of the Ministry do not suggest that there has been or will be any change of direction. In its current reassessment of certification, the Ministry has not considered the possibility of requiring proof that a teacher has maintained contact either with his subject or with new classroom practice. To the extent that *Dimensions*, the Ontario Ministry of Education's newsmagazine, expresses official opinion, one might well conclude that the continuing professional growth of teachers is of little import in the minds of the government. The Ministry seems wedded to an assumption that is hostile to the concept of renewal: once certified competent, forever competent. We doubt that this position can be justified in the climate of the 1970s.

Faculties and colleges of education have played an even more limited role than the Ministry in continuing education. Like many Ministry officials, faculty members have contributed substantially to the professional development programs offered throughout the province, but theirs are individual efforts. As institutions, the colleges have tended to see their job primarily in the context of pre-service training. Traditionally confined to responsibilities for the initial preparation of teachers, they have made little effort to assume a leadership role in continuing education. This indifference to the larger issues in education has been accepted and approved in wider education circles. The MacLeod Report, for example, put continuing education far down the list of priorities for colleges; indeed, it dispensed with the issue in a single paragraph.[2] In the past, teachers and administrators looked to individual faculty members for assistance in running a workshop or a course, but they did not expect the colleges to offer such programs as a matter of policy. Only in recent years have faculties seemed to be emerging from this restrictive cocoon to play a more significant part in the field of continuing education.

The Ministry and the colleges, however, are not the only ones to blame. Teachers also must assume some responsibility for the perpetuation of present inadequacies. Many teachers believe, for example, that teachers in the colleges of education are (at best) ivory-tower theorists and that administrators are (at worst) dunderheads. Virtue and wisdom are to be found only at the grassroots. Teachers are enthusiastic, they will tell you, about professional development. In a recent survey of teachers in London, Ontario, for example, a desire for all forms of professional development stood high on their list of priorities.[3] But, teachers will add emphatically, these must be of the right kind, at the right time, and in the right place.

The trouble is, it is remarkably difficult to determine what teachers mean by the *right* way to organize professional development. Divisions exist within the teaching profession about the kinds of activities that constitute professional growth. In a recent paper, J. W. Greig notes that a survey of 700 Ontario teachers showed that "in a word, they want practical ideas and suggestions."[4] They are interested in *what* to and *how* to, rather than *why* to. Yet we know that many of the more useful concepts in recent educational reform must be understood within an intellectual as well as a practical framework.

Those who have had any experience with continuing education — teachers who attempt to organize it themselves, Ministry personnel, university extension departments, education faculty — all say the same thing: if there is no credit attached to a course, teachers won't touch it. And it is no answer for teachers to reply that "methods" courses and workshops are usually a waste of time. They may be; but most teachers will not support subject updating courses, even when they are run by well-known and able people and organized by teachers themselves. We must recognize, of course, that a good number of teachers do in fact attend noncredit courses every year. Nevertheless, it is common knowledge in education circles that floating a noncredit course is a financial risk of the first order, even when many of the expenses are underwritten through the provision of free facilities and free faculty time.

Teachers can hardly afford to be cavalier about their own professional growth. To cite one recent and dramatic example, A. B. Hodgetts found that the teaching of Canadian studies in the schools across the country was an unmitigated disaster. The responsibility for the mess was not laid at the feet of teachers alone; the universities, the colleges of education, and the curriculum planners were all found guilty. But the fact remains that the teachers themselves had done little to improve their own knowledge of the subject. Here is what Hodgetts found:

> Twenty-three percent of our respondents frankly said they had no interest in any outside reading associated with Canadian studies; another 43 percent could not find or make the time for it; 14 percent claimed a certain

amount of outside reading but when prompted could not name anything specific; only 20 percent were making a determined effort to keep abreast of the literature in their field of work. . . . All of our evidence suggests that about four of every five teachers of Canadian studies do not maintain a contemporary intellectual interest in their academic work.[5]

Hodgetts's findings are condemning enough. But another question lurks in the background. Is there any evidence to show that the situation is any different in most other subject areas — in English, mathematics, or science?

What have the teachers' own organizations — the Ontario Secondary School Teachers' Federation, for example — done to encourage their members to keep up with their subjects and their classroom practice? Some OSSTF executive members are certainly concerned. The issue has been raised within the Committee on Teacher Training and Supply and by some local delegates to the Federation's annual assembly. OSSTF spends a substantial amount of money on a variety of professional development projects, but it is not clear that the majority of its members, or its executive, would support any form of compulsory updating or regular recertification. (And, let it be noted, if exhortation and calls to professionalism were enough, Hodgetts would not have found what he did.)

Indeed, judging from *The Bulletin*, OSSTF's newsletter, one can only conclude that the issue of continuing education is of no interest at all to either the OSSTF executive or the membership. Between 1969 and 1973, a period of four years, *The Bulletin* contained the following considerations of professional development:

October 1969: One article on in-service education; two pages on the specifics of classroom intervisitation

December 1970: One article, of the uplift variety, about keeping abreast of the world generally — which one would expect any educated person to do without exhortation

March 1972: One humorous article about a professional development day spent in a bog

There are important historical reasons why those involved in the profession have not developed a thorough and continuing program of professional development. And teachers are not alone in tackling the problem: updating and upgrading have become issues of concern in all professions. But if one discounts attempts to meet minimum certification standards — an effort that absorbed a tremendous amount of energy in the 1960s — it is difficult to avoid the conclusion that teachers, like most other people, do not take continuing education very seriously. We believe it is a good idea, but we don't exert ourselves to promote it.

Some will argue that continuing education needs can best be met through the extension of graduate work. Graduate work is important and valuable, but it is not in itself the answer to the need for professional development. Aside from the immediate financial and administrative problems connected with a full-scale expansion of graduate programs, the fact remains that graduate work, like the undergraduate degree and pre-service training, is a one-shot affair. It only gives a new dimension to the once certified–always certified syndrome. If graduate programs simply serve as one more rung on a certification ladder, they will not meet the continuing education needs of the 1970s.

Thus far, we have stated that continuing education needs have changed over the last few years. More and more teachers are already fully certified when they begin their careers. The views about continuing education traditionally held by the Ministry, by faculties of education, and by teachers' organizations seem inappropriate and outdated. Old programs at best meet secondary needs and at worst channel our expectations into a dead end. Only a minority of teachers wish to enter areas of new interest, such as guidance, special education, and administration. We can look forward to a period in which all newly certified teachers will have a thorough background and training. How, then, can we provide for renewal? How can we meet in an ongoing way the needs of competent, trained professionals who want to stay in the classroom? How can we provide for a continuing discussion and analysis of general educational issues, curriculum development, changes in subject matter, and teaching strategies?

Recent experience at the University of Western Ontario may throw some light on an alternative approach. For some years it has been clear to members of the faculty of Althouse College that the existing framework for professional development is not satisfactory. Weaknesses in current Ministry policy have been noted, as well as gaps in the range of alternatives available to the fully trained teacher. In the search for alternative systems, the regional approach has emerged as the only means of satisfying present needs.

In undertaking the herculean tasks implied in the concept of renewal, a combined effort by many organizations will be required. At present, responsibility for continuing education rests in many hands — teachers' organizations, local boards, the Ministry, university extension departments, education faculties, OISE local offices, and so forth. There is little coordination of effort and often no communication among the various groups concerned. Local school administrators generally do not know what is being done in the next county, let alone further afield, and the colleges know even less. The time has come to coordinate all these bodies on some kind of regional basis, allowing for considerable flexibility in each area of the province. It is likely that some kind of coordinating committee will be required in each region.

What will make the regional grouping work? How can we ensure that a regional approach will be effective? Three steps in particular must be considered: first, some teaching certificates for the qualified teacher may be made renewable; second, new approaches to cooperative funding within the region will be necessary; and third, many bodies within the region will find themselves in new roles. We will briefly explain each of these points.

The concept of a renewable teaching certificate understandably causes great concern to teachers' professional organizations. It raises the specter of threats, harassment, and firing. But surely it is possible both to avoid these dangers and to achieve very extensive benefits. It may not be necessary or practicable to renew the *basic* qualification of every teacher. An acceptable approach might be to require some evidence of renewal at regular stages in a teacher's career. Certificates granted beyond basic qualification (Type A for secondary school teachers, for example) could be given for limited periods.

It is quite clear that continuing education cannot persist under existing financial arrangements. Serious professional programs in the area require a realigned and coherent system of support. Economies may be achieved through a regional approach in which priorities are rearranged, and available personnel could be used more efficiently and effectively. In short, a regional approach would rationalize the financial aspects of this enormous task in teacher education.

Finally, a regional approach will require institutions within the area to undertake new roles. Teachers' organizations might introduce teacher centers on the British model. Small groups of teachers, education consultants, and other experts could be formed on an ad hoc basis to introduce innovative programs in particular schools or to solve local problems as they arise. Universities and their associated education faculties might make more extensive use of library and human resources. Whatever the pattern, however, the interests of the teachers in the region should come first. At the University of Western Ontario, the faculty are attempting to generate local cohesion and community action through the appointment of a faculty coordinator and a small publication.

Conclusion

The concept of renewal implies the creation of a variety of models to meet regional needs. A recent report by the Professional Education Project indicates the remarkable number of different approaches developed recently for providing continuing education in several professions.[6]

Our argument in this paper has been that the pursuit of continuing education follows no single path and that there is no easy road to realization. Each regional planning group will have to design particular programs to meet the expressed needs of local teachers. In one sense, only the practitioners themselves will know what they require in the immediate future. In another sense, however, the regional planning group will be responsible for *creating* interests and needs. Teachers may be interested primarily in the detail of classroom practice; but problems of epistemology, psychology, and pedagogy are inextricably linked to practice, and teachers who lack some understanding of the larger issues are reduced to mere technicians, vulnerable to faddism and to decisions made by others who have the advantage of more information. A regional concept for continuing education should be developed, not just in terms of service, but also in terms of leadership and intellectual growth.

We suggest, therefore, that a regional — and cooperative — approach to the continuing education of teachers is the most promising course of action. It looks forward, rather than back, and at the same time builds on past achievements. It raises the possibility of a more convincing commitment to excellence in the continuing education of teachers. With regional support of in-service programs, some of the incredibly complex problems inherent in any attempt to reach large numbers of teachers will be capable of resolution. It is an exciting prospect and a challenging one, and it is worth the risks involved in any large-scale revision of the present system.

NOTES
1. James T. Sanders, "Good Teaching — A Disjunctive Concept," *Teacher Education* 5 (Spring 1972): 14–19.
2. The MacLeod Report, p. 48.
3. London Board of Education, "Task Force on Educational Alternatives," mimeographed (November 1972). See especially pp. 11 and 19.
4. J. W. Greig, "Some Remarks about Continuing Education," mimeographed (University of Toronto, Faculty of Education, November 24, 1972).
5. A. B. Hodgetts, *What Culture? What Heritage? A Study of Civic Education in Canada* (Toronto: Ontario Institute for Studies in Education, 1968), p. 108.
6. *The Advancement of Professional Education in Canada: Report of the Professional Education Project* (Toronto: Kellogg Foundation — Ontario Institute for Studies in Education, 1973).

PART TWO

Some Innovative Programs

Teacher Education: Soufflé de fromage, or Cheese Omelet?

Myer Horowitz

For most of my years in education, I have wondered about the components of programs for the preparation of teachers — particularly about the place of the field experience component in the total mix. What are the essential parts of teacher education programs, and how are they to be blended together?

Actually, my interest in *mixing things together* preceded my entry into the teaching profession by about five years. With the help of an uncle who knew the owner, I embarked on my first job at the age of thirteen. It was an after school and weekend job in a restaurant. During the week, I specialized in waiting on tables and preparing caramel sundaes, but occasionally I observed the chef.

I was fascinated the first time I saw the chef prepare a cheese soufflé. It seemed so very simple as he mixed the butter, the flour, the milk, the cheese, the eggs — so simple, yet that night when I mixed the same ingredients, I produced no prize-winning soufflé. My concoction was much closer to a sad-looking omelet. I learned subsequently that simply to use a better brand of cheese would not result in a soufflé. Nor was the answer to include more cheese, or to add the cheese after the eggs rather than before. More than a mechanical formula of ingredients, the success of the soufflé seemed to depend on some rather subtle process and style of blending and preparing its elements.

I was to face the same problems of blending and preparing when I became involved in teacher education. This was especially so when I

This paper is based in part on presentations at conferences sponsored by the Western Canada Association on Student Teaching in Edmonton in March 1972 and by the Ontario Education Association in Toronto in May 1972.

became involved in an effort to institute a new program for a select group of student teachers at McGill University in the fall of 1967.[1] My approach was certainly influenced by the research I had done on student teaching in the early 1960s,[2] but of even more importance was a personal experience. In the autumn of 1966, I had an unfortunate illness that resulted in my being hospitalized for more than five weeks. While the first few days were unpleasant, the latter part of the five-week period was interesting because I was able to do a lot of reflecting. I also had worthwhile discussions with a number of physicians and nurses who were very much involved in medical and nursing education.

I observed what was going on in the ward, and I noticed a number of things. I recall that one of my first contacts after I regained consciousness was with an attractive young woman who tiptoed into the room and asked, "Are you awake, Dr. Horowitz?" I think I smiled as she watered the plant; I know I wanted to.

She did not appear the next day, nor the day after that; but about a week later, she came back again. I learned that she had started her nursing education program just three weeks earlier and that her half-day each week on the wards during the first few months represented her orientation to nursing. I watched her on successive Thursday mornings and noted her progression from watering plants to tidying beds to making beds. Each week she seemed more confident than she had been the week before in her contacts with the other patients and myself.

One day I discussed with a number of young doctors the preparation they had had in a variety of medical schools. While there were some interesting differences, it became clear that in none of the programs was there a *course* called "student doctoring." Doctors do not talk about "field experience" as something apart from the remainder of the program. Future doctors study pediatrics and surgery and internal medicine. It is inconceivable that they could complete their study of pediatrics without spending a relatively long period in hospitals working with young children and the parents of young children, and yet that experience in the hospitals is not given a special label; it is just part of learning pediatrics.

That caused me to wonder. To what extent had we teacher educators created two worlds, two solitudes, by thinking of the field experience in teacher education as something different and very much apart from everything else that was going on? To what extent had we conditioned teachers in the field and student teachers to look upon student teaching as an experience not too closely related to the remainder of the program? How many student teachers are advised by practicing teachers in the schools to ignore much of what is taught in teachers' colleges or in faculties of education?

Project MEET

As a result of my analysis of the major problems of teacher education, and with my hospital experience very much in mind, I prepared a proposal for a different program of preparation. This became the basis for Project MEET (McGill Elementary Education Teaching-Teams), instituted in the fall of 1967.[3] In my original draft, which I circulated to my colleagues, I included a number of my tentative beliefs —

1. that it is worthwhile to explore team relationships in teaching at both the public school and the university levels;
2. that student teachers learn in part from participating with professional teachers in planning, in teaching, and in evaluating;
3. that there is value in a pattern for the preparation of teachers that places emphasis on practice in the schools;
4. that the approach to the various foundations of education should be an interrelated one and that the foundations should be closely related to methodology and practice;
5. that students learn to become teachers when their theoretical and practical experiences are concurrent;
6. that curriculum development is as necessary in teacher education as in the elementary and secondary schools;
7. that the primary responsibility for the preparation of teachers rests with the university faculty of education, but that the school systems and their teachers and administrators should be encouraged to cooperate in planning, executing, and evaluating the program;
8. that a faculty of education has a responsibility to school systems in assisting them in curriculum development and in school reorganization, but that the faculty's contribution is enhanced when interns of the faculty are in these cooperating schools;
9. that before major changes are introduced in teacher education affecting all students, some exploration is necessary with a small group of one classification of student.

These were some of the notions we tried to incorporate and test in the McGill program. Nineteen students, all university graduates, were involved. These interns participated in lectures and seminars on the campus on Mondays and Fridays, and they were assigned to schools for Tuesdays, Wednesdays, and Thursdays during the academic year, as well as for five days each week from the middle of May to the end of June. They were supervised both by teachers in the schools and by college supervisors. Each intern was awarded a bursary by the school system to which he was assigned.

The principal of each cooperating school was asked to involve the intern as a member of the professional staff. Some schools developed teams that included a leader and teachers from a number of grade levels. In other schools, where the interns were assigned to two or more teachers of a particular grade, the team teaching or cooperative teaching patterns evolved very gradually. It was considered essential that each school be given the opportunity to develop its own way of involving interns, because it was felt that an imposed structure would not necessarily result in the kind of change we were interested in achieving.

There were two related major objectives in this project. The first was to explore the possibilities of internship patterns in teacher education; the second was to make some contribution to practice in the schools by encouraging curriculum development and school reorganization.

While we placed emphasis on learning by becoming involved in the classrooms and schools, we also considered it crucial for students to reflect on their school experience when they returned to the campus. Too often the opportunity to review student teaching experience is omitted from proposals for longer periods in the schools.

We watched the program carefully during the 1967/68 year. One of the graduate students conducted a study under my direction on the changes in attitudes and expectations on the part of the interns during their year of teacher education.[4] We employed a number of measuring instruments, such as the Minnesota Teacher Attitude Inventory, and the Teacher Role Description, an instrument that I had previously developed.[5] More important than these measures, however, were the interns' anecdotal records and papers and the results of interviews in depth with a professional counselor who had no previous involvement in the project. As many would predict, we found that the attitudes of interns toward teaching were more positive after their year of teacher education. This finding simply confirmed what had been reported on numerous previous occasions.

The newness of the program seemed to be an important factor in shaping the attitudes of interns. The people involved in the project wanted it to succeed. This was as true for the teachers and principals in the schools as it was for the students and their instructors at the university. The interns in many ways considered themselves to be privileged and part of a select group.

In conversation with the professional counselor, the interns indicated that they placed a great deal of importance on the way they were treated by other people. They considered the relationships with supervisors, instructors, and people in the schools to be "healthy." Several students indicated that there had been a constant dialogue between the interns and the supervisors at university. One intern suggested that because he was treated on an equal basis, he felt like a mature adult. Their contributions in the schools helped the interns to perceive themselves as responsible teachers rather than students.

Each Friday morning, following the three days in school, the interns met with me in an advisory group session. One of the interns labeled these "group therapy" sessions. We soon discovered that this hour each week, where interns shared with each other their challenges, successes, and disappointments, was an essential component of the program.

The small size of the group in the initial year of the program enabled the interns to get to know each other, and the interns and faculty instructors and supervisors came to understand one another personally as well as professionally.

The interns were pleased with what they considered to be valuable flexibility in the program, but, as several of them emphasized, they were referring primarily to the program in the context of the schools rather than of the university. At the school level, individual programs in teacher preparation evolved. The interns spoke of their workload at the school as "reasonable, flexible, and self-imposed." To a great extent, the interns acquired experience in the schools at their own speed and in areas of their own choice.

These were some of the successes, but it is appropriate to deal as well with the problems that developed. Too often we become so enamored with experimental programs that we look only for successes and forget that sometimes the greatest contribution they can make is to illuminate the problems involved.

The lack of flexibility of the program on the campus was serious. Although there were changes in the number of required courses and in the time devoted to each course, there were few fundamental changes in the curriculum of the formal courses — and we soon learned what we already should have known; that you cannot change one part of the program (field experiences) without reshaping the remainder of the program as well.

We felt that the school should develop its own particular translation of the general model of teacher preparation but, with every good intention, we leaned too heavily in the direction of decision making at the school and classroom levels. Several of our colleagues in the field indicated at the end of the year that, in their judgment, we did not give them any guidelines at all.

The follow-up data I have collected more recently support these earlier findings. One year after they were teaching, we asked each of the nineteen interns to complete and return a questionnaire. We also invited them to dinner at the campus and so were able to meet them and discuss the program with them in a more personal way.

After their first year of teaching, many of these people continued to place a great deal of importance on human contacts. This is what one of the interns wrote in the spring of 1969:

> At this time I would like to single out a feature of the MEET Project that was obviously designed—this is the team aspect of the program. Individuals, when on their own, usually have only so much strength and initiative, but when people work together much is gained.
>
> It was obvious that the people responsible for the program believed this and so they introduced a program that used teams in the cooperating schools and at the college. Interns and teachers were able to work together even in settings where teachers had not actively cooperated with other teachers. In established team teaching schools interns also were accepted and used to enrich a functioning unit. At the college the interns became a team: an entity so strong that the interns have been oblivious of the hundreds of other students around them at all times.

Another intern emphasized the extent to which interns helped each other in making the transition from student role to teacher role:

> During the first part of the internship I was confused as to what "role" I should assume. Was I a student or was I a teacher? I had difficulty, at times, in rationalizing my existence as either.
>
> Around me were eighteen other people facing the same problem, to a greater or lesser extent. Those interns who, within themselves, had overcome the student vs. teacher role conflict were of great help to the others. All that was needed was a forlorn sigh at the lunch table. What may have kept many of us going were these informal group therapy lunches.
>
> To me, one of the reasons for the success of MEET stemmed from the "one for all and all for one" feeling among the interns. I will leave it to the experts to attempt an answer for the existence of this closeness. As for myself, in retrospect, the other interns had a valuable influence on my creative and professional development. I see the interns themselves as the first force on my development.

Some emotional stress was revealed during the year of preparation, but we became more aware of this after we met with the interns a year later:

> I remember having a preconceived notion of how things would be, and how perfectly Project MEET would suit me, and now, having completed my internship I again believe this to be true. Now, why do I say "again"? Simply because on occasions during my internship I did not believe this to be true. I don't believe I ever before went through such a gambit of emotions as during that year. All of us, not just interns, used to talk of the "down swings" and the "up swings" in our experiences, and how valuable both are in the development of an individual. Yet, in the midst of those "down swings," what one of us wouldn't have liked to say, "To hang with my development, just get me out of this situation!" But most of us didn't, for with the support of our MEET family, we survived these "crises."

This intern is reminding us that if by *internship* we mean that we simply place students in the schools for longer periods of time with few opportunities for them to relate to and cooperate with one another, we may create more problems than we solve. We must think through very carefully the kind of *help* these people need so that growth and maturity will be the outcome of their experiences.

I referred earlier to the important Friday sessions. One of the interns emphasized this part of the program:

> Fridays became rather important days during that short period of time that we spent at the College. Their importance came about because of the very special meetings that were scheduled. Indeed we cannot forget how we became so closely knit together to the extent that we shared equally the joys as well as the miseries of each member of the group—a thing that is with us until now and will remain with us for a long time.

I think it is important to emphasize what this intern said. Some teacher educators fear that placing new importance on learning by becoming involved in schools will detract from learning at the university center. I think that this need not necessarily be the case. There was a spirit of academic growth:

> Wonderful new horizons seem continually to be opening up. I enjoyed the study atmosphere of the university, and hope to return to it on a full-time basis in the next few years. For the present, however, I am wholly intent on releasing my energies and pent-up ideas, and working myself to the full limit so that I can make the school year as meaningful as possible to the children I teach. I can now enjoy an ideal balance between research and practical application of what I learn.

Several of the interns suggested that the program affected them personally. One wrote as follows:

> I don't know whether anyone is now in the process of studying the teachers produced by an internship program, but if my opinion were required I would proudly state (though admittedly prejudiced) that I am probably a more spirited and interested teacher than I would have been with a different training. I have carried out my own "introspective" study during the year, and here are my major findings:
> 1. This teacher is a basically shy person, and is usually prone to carrying out ideas and projects independently. However, in her first year of teaching, and after one year's intensive training amidst stimulating and helpful people, she has felt strongly the symptom of "four walls closing in on her" and has taken to peeking into other self-contained classrooms to see what other classrooms look like. She is now a confirmed team-teacher, and sadly misses this aspect of her training program.
> 2. This teacher's colleagues bitterly scorn some of the training they have received, stating that it was a mere "hodge-podge" of ideas and theories. Few had a real opportunity to experiment and gain confidence in what

they learned, as she did. Armed with this belief in the need to have faith in the new thinking, she has not been afraid to broaden the experiences in her own classroom, and has a morbid fear of the rut of routine and habit.
3. Not only unafraid to try the ideas she has seen succeed, this teacher wants to continue being caught up in the onrush of educational advances. She has plans to continue taking professional courses in the summer, and perhaps eventually study for a master's degree. The reading habits that were begun last year have continued, and have greater meaning now. And I truly believe that my keen interest in education was inspired by my so very close contacts with people to whom education was a tremendously vital force.

For me Project MEET was one of the most important experiences in my life.

The Project in Retrospect

To this point, I have selected portions from the many items that were presented to me after the interns' first year of teaching. In the spring of 1971, almost three years after their graduation, the nineteen interns were invited to communicate again, and *all* did. In addition to the questionnaire that they all completed and the letters that most wrote, several interns met me for personal interviews.

While the interns continued to be positive about their preparation, I became more aware of the extent to which this type of experience — where people are learning, living, and teaching in close and continuous contact with other individuals — can result in emotional stress. Three years after the experience, one wrote:

> The necessity of assuming two different roles which at times conflicted with each other and at other times enhanced each other—I found that was at times a challenge and at times a frustration.

When asked to recall problems from the internship year, one replied, "I've repressed too much to remember." When asked if anything that seemed important in 1967/68 was unimportant now, the same intern continued, "The whole experience, to be brutally frank." This intern had a relatively successful first year of teaching:

> At no time did I feel the tremendous pressure that I felt during MEET. In addition, the experience did much to help patch up my tattered ego, still shredded from the previous year.

Naturally, none of us who gave direction to the program wanted this intern to feel inferior; but this is what she perceived, and what she perceived was (and is) real for her. She indicated that she felt very inferior in comparison with the others, and she concluded that she must be maladjusted. Whatever positive value the project had for the majority of interns, for this human being it was not a happy or profitable experience.

Looking back, I must admit that I felt the internship year would eliminate most problems of adjustment during the first year of teaching. I realize now that for many interns the year of preparation may have helped in the transition from student to teacher, but that the major adjustment had not taken place before they assumed their first teaching positions:

> I am not sure that a year is enough to bring about that "change in self perception" from student to teacher—I have needed at least two or three years—and I'm not sure it's complete yet.

Unfortunately, the staffing policies of some school systems contributed significantly to the difficulties these people experienced in their early years of teaching. The principal of one of the schools where an intern was posted emphasized the possible effect of staffing patterns on neophyte teachers:

> The Personnel Department of our Board jealously guards the right to appoint teachers to schools as they see fit. Principals are not consulted. It is obvious that faulty assignments of teachers to schools could very well frustrate, demoralize and even ruin new teacher candidates who have superior teaching potential.

Each of the principals of the schools where the interns were teaching during 1970/71 was invited to write. The following statement is representative of several that were received:

> I have had other young teachers in my school, but none was any more interested and capable than ———. It is difficult to isolate causes which produce results. No doubt ———, being a very bright girl with a vivacious personality and an interest in children and teaching, might have become a good teacher under any type of teacher training program. But certainly the training she received seems to have been very successful.

Further Questions

What does this project have to say about teacher education generally and about internship in particular? I fear that in some places internship is being looked upon as the solution to all the problems in teacher education. Certainly, many of us who have been directly involved in internship approaches are excited about the possibilities. But as I have tried to indicate, while the experience generally was a successful one, there were serious problems. If we are interested in developing quality internship patterns in teacher education, then it becomes necessary to raise a number of issues that may help us to avoid some difficulties.

1. *Definition.* Is an internship simply a longer period in the school, or does it imply particular experiences, special relationships between the intern and the staff at the university and in the schools, and payment for

service? Must it follow basic preparation (as in medical education), or can it be part of the undergraduate degree program? To what extent is the organization of the internship the responsibility of the profession, the school systems, the department of education, and the university? Who supervises the intern, and how are these supervisors prepared? Should any field experience precede the internship? In what ways do we relate the internship to other parts of the teacher education program?

2. *Integration.* While extended experience in the field may be essential for a quality teacher education program, it is not sufficient. The key issue has to do with the ability of the future teacher to integrate what he learns in a variety of settings. This has several major implications. To what extent are the courses in the faculty of education related to those that the student takes outside the faculty? Within the faculty of education, to what extent are the professional courses related to the field experience? For me, this suggests that it is essential for the extended field experience to be seen as part of the total program. Certainly, during the internship period, the interns should come together for seminars on a regular basis so that they can reflect on their experiences.

3. *Sequential experiences.* The future teacher should go through a number of different periods of field experience to help him make the transition from student to teacher. His early experiences should give him an orientation to education in different settings, at a variety of grade levels, and in more than one subject area. No matter how valuable the internship or the extended field experience, the beginning teacher requires special help during his first few years of teaching. A poor initial assignment or a particularly heavy instructional load may crush a first-year teacher.

4. *Supervision.* The nature of the supervision, more than anything else, determines whether the student is experiencing high quality internship or lower level apprenticeship. The intern needs help from sympathetic professionals both in the school and at the university. If the professional studies at the university are to be related to the internship, then staff from the faculty must be involved in the supervision of the students. The major supervisory forces, however, are the teachers and principals in the schools. Too often we assume that a good teacher will automatically be an effective supervisor of student teachers. This is not necessarily the case. Cooperating teachers deserve help in preparing for the supervisory role.

5. *Cooperative planning.* While the primary responsibility for the preparation of teachers belongs to the faculty of education, school systems and their teachers and administrators must be involved in developing the program.

6. *Interaction.* New approaches will have positive results only if people are able to relate directly with each other. The group of interns should be sufficiently small so that it is possible for the interns to know each other well. Peers often represent the major influence group for the intern. Whether or not he can identify with other interns and get support from them may seriously affect the value of his experience.

Let me return to my interest in soufflés. Recently I examined a number of cookbooks. The recipe for soufflé in the *Encyclopaedia of Cooking* was different from the one the cook used in the restaurant where I worked in the 1950s. This recipe recommended the use of three tablespoons of butter, not two; five tablespoons of flour, not six. The instructions emphasized that it was absolutely essential to blend the butter and the flour before adding the hot milk. My mentor, the cook, added hot milk *first;* yet his soufflé, too, was superb.

Larousse gastronomique, a recognized authority in the cooking field, advocated even more variation; and James Beard included, in addition to the usual ingredients, a half-teaspoon of tabasco. He insists the tabasco is absolutely essential.

Obviously, there are many ways of preparing soufflés. It is agreed by most of the authorities that certain of the ingredients are important, and that some are absolutely essential, but there is little agreement as to the quantity of each of these components, or the order of mixing.

Many specific program plans in teacher education can be developed. Whether the field experience should be six weeks or twelve, whether it should be three days a week or five, and whether it should be in the spring of the third year of university or in the fall of the fourth year are important questions; but they are far less crucial than the need to develop a total teacher education program that will enable the future teacher, with help from professionals in the schools and at the university, to *integrate* what he learns into his developing concept of the role of the teacher.

We can increase the amount and improve the quality of the cheese and the eggs (and the arts and science, foundations, curriculum and instruction, and field experience components); but if we haven't given a great deal of thought to putting the pieces together in a harmonious mix, then the intended gourmet *soufflé de fromage* may emerge as a flat and uninspired cheese omelet.

NOTES

1. The project continued for four years. Since I was involved only for the first two years, I shall be referring primarily to that experience.

2. See M. Horowitz, "Role Relationships in Student Teaching Settings" (Ph.D. diss., Stanford University, 1965) and "Student-Teaching Experiences and Attitudes of Student Teachers," *Journal of Teacher Education* 19 (1968): 317–24.

3. M. Horowitz, "Project MEET," *McGill Journal of Education* 2 (1967): 183–85.

4. See H. Nichol, "An Internship Programme in Teacher Education and Its Effect on the Attitudes of Interns" (master's thesis, McGill University, 1968).

5. Included in Horowitz, "Role Relationships."

A Concurrent Program in Scotland

J. H. Duthie

No one is in a position to make recommendations about the most effective way to educate teachers unless he has tried out his proposals, evaluated the results, and compared his program with the various possible alternatives. Intriguing ideas are plentiful in this field,[1] and variety in teacher education programs certainly should be encouraged. But unless these imaginative proposals are carefully and systematically tested and assessed, we shall be no more able to reach firm conclusions about which strategies are most effective in preparing teachers than we are at present. At the moment, the evidence is so lacking that we are forced to rely largely on hunches and intuition.

Like most people in the field, I have my own strong preferences and prejudices. If we are to move beyond personal opinion, however, we must pay more attention to evaluating what we do in teacher education. This evaluation should take place on at least two levels. Within various organizational and course settings, particular approaches or techniques may be used, and these should be carefully assessed. Microteaching, for example, is a component of many teacher education programs, particularly in the United States.[2] Indeed, a considerable amount of evaluation work has been done in teacher education projects of this sort.

Besides evaluating the component parts of teacher education programs, we must also attempt to assess the effectiveness of the overall organizational context and philosophical approach of the programs themselves. This is a much more complex and difficult task, but it is nonetheless essential. To illustrate the difficulties, I shall describe a program

---

I would like to acknowledge the help and advice of Ken Kennedy, who read an early draft of this paper and provided many valuable suggestions.

of teacher education in which I have been involved at Stirling University in Scotland. This program has been in operation for five years; and although we have spent the greater part of our time and effort on implementing it — and in teaching — about a dozen papers have been produced examining and evaluating various aspects of the program.[3] From these, it is hoped, will emerge a better overall assessment of the strengths and the weaknesses of the Stirling program.

The University of Stirling is unique among Scottish universities in offering a *concurrent* teacher education program, combining over a period of years undergraduate study of academic subjects commonly taught in schools, the study of education, and professional preparation for prospective teachers. As in Ontario, the Scottish tradition of teacher education at the university level has been entirely in the consecutive mold, with the student first of all studying for an academic degree and then taking a postgraduate qualification of one year.

Although the pattern of the Stirling program is unusual in the Scottish context, its contents and methods when we started were conventional enough, apart from the inclusion of microteaching. At first, microteaching was merely tacked onto conventional courses in psychology, sociology, and methods, but it soon became clear that if we were to make use of the opportunities afforded by microteaching, it had to be tied in much more closely with the theoretical aspects of the course.

The first, and admittedly crude, evaluation of the course indicated to us that all was not well. That evaluation was in the form of falling student numbers. The course that replaced it and that has now been running for two years involves a much tighter integration of theory and practice. Psychology is seen as providing a theoretical context for the understanding and practice of microteaching skills. As far as possible, only those aspects of psychology are taught that are directly relevant to the business of learning to be a teacher. In conventional courses, psychology tends to be only tenuously related to teaching. Our aim is to help students to understand the theory behind teaching skills.

Microteaching provides the backbone of the first-year course. During the first semester, students practice various cognitive skills, chiefly centering around questioning — questioning for feedback, higher order questioning, and so on. The practice of each of these skills is preceded by lectures on related theory; for example, the skill of higher order questioning is preceded by three lectures on Piaget's distinction between concrete and formal operations, and a fourth lecture introducing the skill and providing practice in the use of an assessment procedure. In the following weeks, students practice the skill in a microteaching situation. Having planned their lesson, they teach it for a period of twelve minutes to a group of five pupils brought in from local secondary schools (the children are twelve to thirteen years of age). The lesson is videotaped, and the students immediately view the recording along with a tutor. Then they replan the lesson and reteach it for a further twelve minutes to another group of five children. On the second occasion, they view the videotape either alone or, if they prefer it, with other students from the class. We would prefer to provide tutors on both occasions, but because of increasing numbers, we find it necessary to restrict their use to the first teaching session only. (It should be noted that a recent evaluative study we made indicates that students make as effective tutors as academic staff. This potential economy, however, is not as attractive as it might appear, because the study also indicated that student morale is higher when academic staff are present.)

The second semester is geared to a study of class control and motivational techniques.[4] Part of this course is taught through the use of an individualized instruction package based on the Far West Laboratory mini-courses. Integrated into this course are microteaching skills related to pupil motivation and class discussion. The second semester microteaching course is paralleled by one that emphasizes lesson planning: this course uses programmed instruction as a paradigm. Students initially learn to construct a linear program; they follow this with the construction of branching programs and, finally, of individualized instruction packages. As they devise and test these programs, students learn to anticipate pupil responses and difficulties and so move from the "interactive" microteaching situation to the longer-term considerations of lesson planning.

In the third semester of education, major attention is given to helping students transfer the microteaching and planning skills they have learned to the classroom situation. For a full semester, students practice teaching lessons to a class of about fifteen pupils whom they meet once a week for ten weeks. This course leads into the first secondary school teaching practice between the third and fourth semesters of education. During semesters two and three, students also attend curriculum tutorials in which they meet and converse with tutors who are specialists in their own school teaching subject. When they return from the first secondary teaching practice, students make a study of wider educational issues, such as the sociology of the school and philosophical questions.

In their introductory course, then, students concentrate on the theory and practice of interaction with small groups of pupils — a "shallow-end" approach to the problems of learning to be an effective teacher. Thereafter, students are gradually introduced to longer-term and more general considerations. As the course progresses, it thus opens up in a number of ways. Students initially study and practice small-scale interaction with a small group of pupils for short periods of time. Gradually the scale of these encounters is increased, until a year and a half later they are giving full-length lessons to full-sized classes in schools. Later still, the course broadens out yet again to include general educational issues. Again, students start by short-term planning of simple interaction with pupils; gradually longer-term considerations of lesson planning are introduced; and later still, issues in educational philosophy are studied. The rationale for the course, then, is that we should introduce students at the beginning of the course to those problems that they can see and cope with, and only gradually introduce broader and deeper issues as the students become competent to deal with them.

A number of research students in the university's Department of Education have taken as their dissertation topic the evaluation of particular aspects of the course. Other studies are being undertaken by faculty members. Some of these studies are of the conventional control-group sort — for example, comparing the effectiveness of video and audio feedback in relation to different microteaching skills. It is not necessary, or indeed appropriate, for all evaluation to be of this kind. In setting up a course such as ours, where not only one's methods but one's objectives differ considerably from those in other training institutions, it is more appropriate simply to state one's objectives, to develop means for achieving these, and to evaluate whether one has, by these means, realized the objectives. Much of the evaluation of a course of this sort must inevitably — and rightly — be in this form.

I am not suggesting that a rigid or mechanistic evaluation system be applied relentlessly to all components and all programs in teacher education. What I am advocating is a more conscious and systematically critical assessment of these enterprises. Our evidence will come from many sources — students, faculty members, practicing teachers, school children, parents — and will take many forms. But unless we give major and continuing attention to soliciting, gathering, exchanging, and carefully analyzing such evaluative information, we will surely have no grounds on which to make any claims about the relative effectiveness or merits of one approach or program in comparison with another.

NOTES

1. See, for example, *Concepts in Teacher Education* (Toronto: Ontario Teachers' Federation, 1971).

2. One example is the series of mini-courses being produced at the Far West Laboratory for Educational Research and Development in Berkeley, California. The *Report of the Minister of Education, Ontario, 1969* (Toronto:

Ontario Department of Education, 1970), p. 6, makes it clear that there is also an increasing emphasis on microteaching in the Ontario teachers' colleges.

3. See, for example, D. McIntyre and J. Duthie, "Students' Reactions to Microteaching," and C. Millar and D. McIntyre, "The Analysis of Students' Evaluation of Observed Teaching." (Typescripts available on request.)

4. Since this article was written, and as a result of the kind of evaluation it advocates, the first and second semester courses have been interchanged.

The Implications of In-Service Programs

Donald Longwell

People with talent can make far-reaching impressions upon us. Our enthusiasm for similar achievements for ourselves is stimulated by their example. As we listen or watch, we imagine ourselves in the winner's circle too. Then, with renewed ambition, we turn to new endeavors. As a boy watching a hockey game, I was greatly impressed by the prowess of players of my own age. From this experience came the initial drive that later led to long hours of practice on the basketball court and to great enjoyment in playing that game. Competence in any form can encourage us to acquire new skills and to achieve greater self-development. Whether or not such endeavors always succeed may not be very important. The involvement and the attempt are usually well worth the effort.

I feel that a successful teacher must have this effect on other people. The motivation for learning seems to be strongly encouraged by the example of and through contact with people who are both skilled in what they are doing and enthusiastic about it. This theme might be worth keeping in mind when we consider the education of teachers in Ontario.

There are two separate kinds of teacher education in Ontario. One type consists of a *pre-service* period, usually a year, spent in a teachers' college or a university faculty of education. These pre-service programs tend to be formal, rigid, and institutionalized, despite many curriculum innovations. In the judgment of many student teachers, and indeed of many practicing teachers, most pre-service programs are a waste of time.

The great majority of students have accepted this evaluation before they come to the teachers' college. During the year, the chief complaints, frequently expressed with considerable malevolence, are that students are treated like children, that the curriculum is irrelevant and out of touch, and that staff are incompetent. This ill-natured, often rancorous, spirit may color all facets of life at the college. There are, of course, staff of unquestioned talent and curriculum programs of obvious value to a prospective teacher. But the influence of an atmosphere compounded of fear, tension, and futility is strong. The great potential of this period of teacher preparation has yet to be realized.

Is pre-service teacher education really a waste of time? For many student teachers, it most certainly is. It is as easy to enroll at a teachers' college as it is difficult to get hired by a board of education a year later. The college attracts those who have nowhere else to go: refugees from the business world, bored housewives, hopeless idealists with a pass arts B.A., misfits and fugitives from life's many skirmishes — people, in short, who have come into teaching as the last resort of the incompetent. At the other extreme, however, there are the individuals with enough creative talent, drive, and dedication to equip a regiment of ordinary pedagogues. They are exceptional student teachers, with more to offer the college than they have to gain from it. No further preparation is needed; except for their teaching certificate, they are ready for the classroom. Between these two groups are the great number of individuals whose capacity for teaching is unknown, even to themselves. To them, a year of preparation can be helpful. There is no doubt that many student teachers benefit from their pre-service year of teacher education. But some do not, and — what is worse — a few of them actually emerge with their personal outlook on children and the school system damaged.

The second type of teacher education in Ontario is more informal and diverse. It consists of the many in-service programs offered by boards of education, teachers' federations, professional and commercial organizations, and other agencies involved in the field of education. An important section of the Ministry of Education, the Professional Development section, has organized and supported extensive summer and winter courses for teachers (largely those in elementary schools). Many of these courses have earned a significant measure of success.

As someone who has had experience with both kinds of teacher education, I feel that the latter system, though often denigrated, has provided more opportunities for the qualities of good teaching to flourish.

Hamilton Primary Methods Course (1971)
— "Up! Up! With people!"
— "This week I got a good feeling about myself."
— "I really feel that there is truly a very beautiful, worthwhile individual within me; now if I can only let the S.O.B. out!"

These comments were made by three school teachers enrolled in the Ministry-sponsored 1971 Hamilton Primary Methods summer course.

They were written as part of a continuous teacher evaluation of the curriculum. They reflect very different attitudes from those of the students of the teachers' colleges referred to earlier. This course is only one example of many courses like it. The philosophy and planning underlying such courses can be illustrated by examining in some detail the organization and activities established for the Hamilton course.

The planners envisaged three basic types and areas of activity for the children and adults participating in the course. The first type of activity would take place in a large open area — probably a cafeteria or gymnasium — where a number of "interest centers" and "resource centers" were located. The interest centers would offer a wide range of activities, from arts and crafts to more specialized technical skills, and the resource centers would provide materials of all kinds. The basic purpose of this open area would be to provide a situation where adults and children could work together and relate to each other, not as teachers and students, but as individuals interested in a particular common activity or project. The adults were to have no responsibility for the direction or conduct of the children (the summer course staff would take care of such matters where necessary). It was hoped that they would develop a variety of relationships with each other and with the children in the course of these activities.

A second type of activity was to take the form of more specialized sessions arranged by staff members in the classroom setting. Third, there were to be many outstanding resource people who would visit the course for short periods of time. Demonstration and discussion would take place with school principals, artists, musicians, creative-writing experts, and poets. Along with the presentations dealing with classroom curriculum and related school matters, advice would be offered on how to mix concrete, build a model rocket, construct a telescope for viewing the night sky, print and develop photographs, and survive an overnight camping trip. Throughout the course, it was hoped that the wall so often present between school work and the world at large might be diminished, if not eliminated.

For teachers taking the course, there was always a place to go and something to do. At the same time, there was every encouragement to adapt the existing program to meet their own immediate needs and desires. Timetabling was worked out to fit the requirements of the people and events decided upon. Course time was provided for personal interests, as well as time, resources, and stimulation for efforts which would be of direct and immediate benefit to the classroom.

The kind of organization described above was, in the main, put into effect. It is interesting to note that many teachers who advocate a free and unstructured curriculum find it difficult to cope when they are exposed to one. Some never do. It is not difficult to see why. Conditioned by a structured, teacher-oriented system, they have been teaching as they were taught, and the habit is firmly entrenched. This is the great irony of our pre-service teacher preparation. Fresh from university (second only to high school as a perpetuator of disastrous teaching methods), many student teachers profess with great vigor their commitment to the ideals of a free, student-centered curriculum; then, when exposed to such a curriculum in the classroom and even in some teachers' colleges, they beat a hasty retreat to the comfort of authoritarian, traditional teaching methods.

The Ministry of Education summer course was consciously organized to deal with this problem. There were some indications of a growing awareness of the problem itself if not some signs of success in overcoming it. The following remarks are taken from the course evaluations written by the teachers who were taking the Hamilton Primary Methods course:

— "This type of organization is particularly necessary because the present generation of teachers have mostly been educated in a traditional system and consequently are stuck in the 'generation gap' created by the revolution in education."

— "With no substantial personal experience in the new methodology, it is difficult to incorporate it meaningfully and easily into one's own repertoire."

— "I enjoyed the freedom involved in planning my own timetable."

— "In general, I have found each week seemed to improve as I accepted the freedom for my benefit and went to things that interested me and did things that would be helpful to me."

— "The freedom that was allowed really showed to me the teachers who wanted to be 'spoon fed' and the teachers who came to search, discover, investigate and think for themselves."

— "I found I've got through more interesting professional reading in the past week than I have in the past year! Terrific!"

An important difference between these less formal, more diverse in-service courses and the more formal, massive, institutionalized pre-service courses is the emphasis in the latter on considerations beyond the level of organization and administration. In the Hamilton course, for example, a deliberate and large-scale attempt was made to bring about a greater personal self-awareness. Many participants accepted the invitation to discuss freely their fears, anxieties, and feelings toward themselves and others. All staff members encouraged the free exchange of ideas, impressions, sensations, and feelings of any kind that were a part of the complex associations between an individual teacher and the world he or she traveled in each day. An open, warm, natural, relaxed, friendly, trusting atmosphere emerged through this exchange. A few on the staff, with particular competence in this regard, added much to a growing awareness, on the part not only of individuals, but in a kind of organic way, of the course as a whole. Again, we note some reactions of the course participants:

— "Almost no one teaching the course attempted to intimidate the teachers in favor of their own ideas. Rather, there was an observable and pleasing attempt by the course teachers to accommodate the students' interests and treat them with respect and equality — as professional people."

— "It was a very warm and trustful atmosphere in which everyone shared freely and seemed to gain a better understanding of human relationships."

— "How can I express myself in words? I feel I have gained greater insight into myself, first as a person, secondly as a teacher, thirdly — what a child is — a person — and how to guide and direct him to have a happy enjoyable school experience as a part of life itself."

Evaluations such as these were so extensive that the pressure of being constantly assessed and graded, usually a burden on the student in any teaching situation, was, in this course, a pressure on the staff. This pressure lessened somewhat as teachers writing their evaluations finally began to include more self-evaluation as well as program evaluation —

— "I was asked to look after a four-year-old child. I have one year's experience in grade 1. I did not know what to do with the child."

Little pressure in fact existed in regard to "passing" or "failing." Attendance was taken, but not in a way that constituted a threat or a form of coercion. Administrative procedures were kept to a minimum, worked out to support the demands of the course participants, and effected without loud proclamation. It was felt that too visible and dominant a pressure by the two administrators would hamper the growth of a sense of student direction of the course.

An attempt to respond to the problems and needs that teachers brought to the course necessitated a very flexible organization of alternative activities. To a great extent, teachers taking the course could do their own timetabling. Small groups of course participants, called *families*, worked together, joined other families, or sent representatives to special sessions, depending on their interest or their need. An individual's timetable could be completely self-determined if necessary. Planning for activities that did not fall within the scope of staff presentations was not only encouraged but expected. Many activities occurred that were not a product of staff input.

A great variety of resources (both human and material) was provided to be used by groups of staff and students on independent endeavors as prompted by the felt needs of a particular group:
— "During this week I was more interested in methods and new ideas rather than getting involved with a particular child."
— "I got a lot of ideas that I can use next year."

A crucial component in this course was the participation of a large number of children. Staff members with a background in child-development studies tried, through discussion, to base an interpretation of observations made during the interactions with children on a framework of current thinking in areas of child development. A personal follow-up involving teacher attitudes, fears, and anxieties in response to small children also was encouraged. We note the following remarks:
— "The course has made me more aware of 'the child' rather than 'the lesson.' "
— "The most important thing I got from the course is to try and understand the children in my class better."
— "The course renewed my enthusiasm for children."

Perhaps the most distinctive and significant aspect of the course was its use of a wide variety of resource people whose only qualification was that they were very capable in a particular area. The atmosphere created by this group was, I am convinced, vital to the success of the program. Regular staff members included poets, artists, musicians, scientists, and people from business and industry. Individuals from many walks of life were invited to come to the course and work for a while with teachers. Contact with people who are enthusiastic about what they do can provide a great stimulus. It encourages others, often unconsciously, to turn to their own pursuits with renewed interest and, in many cases, to open new fields of endeavor.

Outstanding teachers, too, can have this effect on their colleagues. Fresh from the classroom, they do not impose their particular style or packaged book of methods. Instead, they strive to make other teachers aware of their individual potential:
— "I feel I have met my first real teacher."
— "This is the kind of speaker that makes you want to get back to your classroom."
— "I came out of his sessions literally inspired!"

A staff of such resource persons is made possible by observing one fundamental principle. *The appointments must be temporary.* They exist for the period of the course only. When the course is over, these people return to their chosen occupation, whether it be predicting the weather, making feature films, or teaching school.

A Proposed Innovation
It is this feature of the summer course program that I believe could be applied successfully to the pre-service teacher education system as well. The gathering together of a group of gifted individuals and a number of young people who wish to become the teachers of children offers exciting possibilities. The core of such a team would be outstanding teachers, supported by some administrators and consultants. The rest of the team, and probably the largest part, would consist of talented, enthusiastic individuals recruited from a wide range of occupations and activities. Again it must be emphasized that the staff appointments would be temporary.

The Ministry of Education would continue its role of assessing the program and certifying its graduates as it saw fit. A small permanent administrative staff at the teacher education institution would undertake to build the core staff for a one-year program. The core staff would be responsible for providing the rudiments of teaching skills and curriculum techniques. It would also take the initiative in recruiting the more diverse personnel necessary to the scheme and with them would plan the details of the program. A number of the staff would serve for more than one year — the program coordinator, in particular, would have to have a two- or three-year term. The basic principle of staffing policy would be to engage a large number of talented and energetic persons, fresh from their involvement in a wide range of activities, in working with students and teachers for varying periods of time.

John Holt was once asked what he would look for in a good teacher. He replied that he would look for a person with a long list. He explained that he had once paused in his own hectic daily rush of speaking and writing to ask himself how many activities he was involved in that were truly creative. He could think of very few. But this, surely, in his view, must be the mark of a good teacher: to be constantly interested in some subject, pursuing some inquiry, building this and trying out that. A good teacher would have a backlog of skills and interests and would always be adding to it. Such a person would have a long list of talents.

The challenge of the teacher education design I have described would, I am sure, spark the enthusiasm of the staff and enlist the support and participation of the students. The aim of the whole enterprise would be, as one teacher at the summer course put it, "to get the idea, the intuitive feeling of education in one's head — not just in a corner of one's room or day book."

As teachers, we are often criticized for being too separate and too well insulated from the world around us. The teacher education institutions seem destined to fill up each year with many people with a common background: university arts experience, no particular talent to offer, and no other place to go. A greater diversity of background is needed.

In many of our in-service teacher education courses, a revolution has been taking place. There is no need to look to other provinces or other countries to borrow and adapt from their programs. We have successful working examples here.

This proposal, if suitably expanded and researched, could benefit by the affiliation between pre-service teacher education and the university curricula. A case also might be made for a non-university setting. Whatever the location, the need for more effective teacher education is critical.

Teachers and Alternative Schools

Robert Beardsley

As more and more boards of education experiment with alternatives to the traditional school, it becomes apparent that teacher training institutions need to consider alternatives in teacher education.

In my opinion, teachers in alternative schools need to be specialists in at least one discipline and generalists in the humanities. They need the same kind of training as those preparing for traditional schools, but in addition they need to take an elective course that could be called "the alternative school option." This course might be described in a calendar as follows:

ALTERNATIVE SCHOOL OPTION
- Readings from the literature on alternative schools.
- Visiting alternative schools in the area, both elementary and secondary.
- Practice teaching in alternative schools.
- A major project consisting of a design for an alternative school, including such matters as aims and objectives, details of plant required, staffing, and admission criteria.

Let me try to justify my opinion by describing the alternative school in which I work and then by describing the teacher's role in that school as I perceive it.

The Toronto Board of Education operates an experimental alternative high school called SEED (Shared Experience, Exploration, and Discovery). It began full-time operation in September 1970. At present, the Board rents space for the school in the YMHA at the corner of Bloor Street and Spadina Avenue in downtown Toronto. It pays the wages of four full-time teachers and three part-time teachers. It also pays for a part-time secretary and provides a modest operating budget.

The original intention of the SEED community — the loose arrangement of parents and students that petitioned the Board for financial support to set up SEED — was to provide a learning climate for highly motivated students who were frustrated by the convoy speed at which they were learning in traditional schools.

In its first year of operation, SEED acquired a mathematics teacher who was seconded from a large technical school. With twenty years in teaching and a variety of experience in mathematics and science to his credit, it was assumed that he could help the students in their search for academic excellence. What SEED had not counted on was that by a process of self-selection, the bulk of the students were anti-science and anti-technology. Consequently, for two months this teacher sat unused in a corner of a ping-pong room, like a dusty reference book in a film library. Day after day he presented himself at SEED, only to find that the blandishments of yoga and Sanskrit and Cantonese were too great for students to resist, particularly in favor of mathematics.

At first he wondered if he should advertise. Perhaps call it "Guerrilla Mathematics" and teach the economics of violent revolution. Perhaps call it "Commune Calculus" and teach rural bookkeeping or health-food calorie counting. Later the teacher wondered if the problem was his lack of fashionable dress or vocabulary, but he concluded in the end he could change neither without being hypocritical.

By November, he had decided to transfer out of the school. He missed his blackboards, he missed his timetabled spares, he had no busy-work to shield him from thinking about what he was doing. He felt naked without all the structures of the traditional school and the buttresses of rank to compensate for his human frailties.

Fortunately for him and his identity crisis, external forces were at work to produce a demand for his services. The students who were taking astrology discovered they needed mathematics to do horoscopes. The budding psychologists found they needed statistics. And strangest of all, some students wearied of the shapelessness that had become a fetish with SEED courses. Like the teacher in question, they realized how much they relied on structure. Students began turning to mathematics and the mathematics teacher.

And then his troubles ended? Not really. For two weeks, he attempted to organize classes and a timetable. It proved almost impossible to arrive at mutually convenient times. Too many things were going on. When he did arrange classes, students would arrive an hour late or on the wrong day. And worse, when he finally achieved a gathering of three people, they were at three different levels. Thoroughly frustrated, he abandoned all attempts at timetabling classes and fell back on a semi-independent study program. And this worked!

In contrast, SEED's language teacher, effervescent and scarcely older than her students, was initially swamped with clients wanting to study languages at all five grade levels. She threw herself into her task, planning lessons, begging books, arranging to borrow visual aids, only to find student attendance shrinking and class attention waning. She too went through a slough of despond. In time, she relaxed. Instead of force-feeding written material, she began concentrating on conversation. She decided to attend foreign language plays and play-readings and to ignore the timetable. She began announcing at the general meeting such things as cancellation of the grade 12 French class because "I'm going to University College to see the French Club perform *Le Malade imaginaire*." Her role changed subtly from that of omniscient teacher to that of excited learner, and the excitement rubbed off. In the fall of 1972 she went back to university and now is teaching at SEED part time. She is assisted by a great many volunteer helpers, and although — to use current jargon — she maintains a low profile, her enthusiasm and drive are essential features in a program that works.

The geography teacher in SEED was a volunteer teacher, a "catalyst" in our lexicon. A parent who had expertise and leisure, she slid into the role quite differently from the two professionals I have just described. Some of her daughter's friends from SEED came to visit, complaining of the lack of geography, and quite voluntarily she came down to the school to see what she could do to help them organize their own grade 13 class, using the Ministry's course outline as a Bible. She never directed and intervened only when a vacuum occurred. The students chose their own topics for seminars that they contracted to give. They asked her for help in assessing their output. They turned to her increasingly for advice and constructive criticism in the actual research. They sought and obtained her cooperation in procuring films and visiting speakers that complemented their seminars and in some cases fleshed out topics that had not captured the interest of students enough to produce a student lecture. In the summer of 1972, this teacher resurrected her credentials from the Ministry of Education, which she had never used, and was subsequently hired as one of the part-time core teachers.

These three case studies indicate the role of the teacher in an alternative school. Of course, resilience and knowledge, enthusiasm and flexibility, empathy and the ability to lead students to lead themselves are qualities to be desired in a traditional school teacher as well; but if they are lacking, a mediocre teacher may be carried by the structures of the school. Unstructured schools provide no such support to the insecure, to the underqualified, or to the inhumane.

I suggested at the outset that an "alternative school option" should include reading, visiting, and practicing teaching. These suggestions are obvious. Less obvious may be the suggestion that the course should include a project involving the design of a model alternative school.

There is some evidence in SEED's third year of operation that the aims and objectives of the school may be shifting. Thus far, there have been no admission requirements other than winning a place by lottery. The school has a maximum registration of 120 students. In 1972/73, there were few students left from the first intake, and the drive for academic excellence shows signs of being on the decline. Perhaps the implementation of the credit system in Ontario high schools has given sufficient freedom of choice to satisfy most students.

There still appears to be a need for SEED, because we continue to get requests for information and applications at the rate of ten to twelve a week. The bulk of these applicants seem to be looking for an emotional retreat. They cannot cope with the tension or the authority structure or peer disapproval in their high school, and they are looking for an alternative. Such an alternative may require different skills than those that our staff team presently possess. Perhaps more guidance skills or social work experience is needed. The point I am trying to make is that just as the individual teachers in an alternative school need flexibility, so too do the alternative schools themselves. They are designed to respond to particular needs or inadequacies in a traditional school system. In theory, they should gradually wither away when they are no longer needed. Teachers in alternative schools, then, need to be constantly on the alert to ensure that their schools are evolving and not simply decaying. They need to be honest and self-critical in order to avoid the trap of parroting their own press-clippings. In short, there is far more need for professionalism in the alternative school teacher than in the traditional; far more need for recognition of the teacher's responsibility for making the system assist the learning process rather than impede it. It is my hope that a project in which a prospective teacher would design a model alternative school, explore its assumptions and implications, and perhaps begin to implement it in a modest way would underline that responsibility. The following paragraphs describe the kind of "alternative school option" I would like to see in teacher education programs.

Probably the best way to learn how to teach in an alternative school is to teach in an alternative school. But the second best, I think, is to try to simulate that experience. What I would propose is a six-week summer program of in-service training, in which teams consisting of five or six student teachers and one counselor would be directed and helped to create and teach a summer program of their own.

Because this would be a simulation, it would probably be necessary for the training school to do some preliminary work, locating physical space in Y's, or churches, or settlement houses, and advertising to attract prospective students. If a mixture and balance of various types of student is considered desirable, some screening of applicants would also be necessary. Beyond this, as much freedom (and responsibility) as they can handle should be thrust upon the student teachers to get the school going.

A team sent to a settlement house in an immigrant area might end up teaching Canadian language, history, and culture to adults. Another team, because of its talents and its location in a downtown Y, might end up running a physical-education-oriented school. A third, in a middle-class suburb, might end up with a focus on the performing arts. Yet another, in a nearby small town, might end up with a sort of outdoor education program. The possibilities are endless.

The counselors, for their part, would need to be flexible enough to accept a great deal of confusion in the first week, while student teachers and clients sorted themselves out. At the end of the first week, I would recommend that the counselors evaluate the overall program. They might have to intervene at this point, because of the limitations of time, sending more teachers to location A or suggesting a student–teacher exchange between locations B and C to ease a personality conflict, but their ultimate goal should be that of enabling learning (and teaching) to go on for at least five weeks. I think the counselors would also have to be prepared for the "failure" or "collapse" of one of their teams for any number of reasons and be able to turn it into a learning experience to be shared by all the teams.

The sixth week would be a period of feedback, sharing of results and experience, and gathering of recommendations for the program in subsequent summers.

Through some such program as this, teacher training institutions could train teachers for work in alternative schools and also help them to recognize equally the reactionary blindness of some critics of alternative schools as well as the romantic blindness of some exponents.

A Role for the Research Scientist

Robert Logan

As an educator, one of the most depressing things I find about our present educational system is the existence of artificial barriers between the different components of the system. The separation of the high school and the university is one example. The separation of high school science students from scientists is another. I wish to propose a simple scheme whereby these two barriers could be overcome. It entails the creation of a new position in which a person spends half his time teaching at the high school and the other half doing research at the university. Before going into the details of my proposal, I shall present a short history of the idea.

It began in 1968 when I, as an American, started teaching physics to first-year students at the University of Toronto. I wanted to understand their background as well as the nature of Ontario high schools, particularly at the grade 13 level, with which I was unfamiliar. So I asked a friend who taught at a Toronto secondary school to invite me out to see what I could learn. I was invited to teach class for the day and had, much to my delight, a very stimulating exchange with the students.

I decided not to prepare any formal lessons, but instead tried to discuss my research in a language that the students could understand — that is, in English, not equationese. The enthusiasm of the students made me realize the potential importance of direct contact between high school students and research scientists. This was a lesson similar to one I had learned previously, at cocktail parties: people were anxious to learn about my research when I could convey it in a language they understood. As a result of my experience in my friend's school, I tried to interest graduate students at the University of Toronto in the concept of a combined career of research and high school teaching. At that time, when university positions were easy to come by, I could not find any interest, possibly because no one wanted to take the risk of doing something for the first time.

About a year and a half later, I learned about SEED, an experimental high school sponsored by the Toronto school board. I decided to put my idea into practice and volunteered to teach physics there once a week for two hours, which I have done now for the past two years. Since the students at SEED are oriented primarily toward the arts, I decided to teach a nonmathematical course the first year to arouse their interest. The course was well attended (by nearly one-third of the school), and the general aim of interesting the students in physics by conveying an understanding of the basic concepts was achieved. By sacrificing the mathematical approach to make the course more relevant, we were able to create more interest in physics than would be possible in the standard high school course. In the second year at SEED I taught a straightforward mathematically oriented grade 13 physics course to many of the same students. The achievement of the students was most gratifying. They grasped *both* the physics and the complicated mathematics concepts taught. I was particularly proud of one student who achieved 680 out of 800 on the American College Board physics exams, a very fine showing indeed.

From my SEED experience, two conclusions emerged. First, there is a need in the high school curriculum for a nonmathematical approach to physics, so that those students who are nontechnically oriented can learn the ideas and concepts of physics and, in some cases, be motivated to do mathematical physics with enthusiasm. Second, there seems to be a definite role for the research scientist in the high school.

By early 1971, I felt that it might be possible to begin to develop such a role and to bridge the gap between scientific research and high school teaching. Accordingly, I made a proposal to the Metropolitan Toronto School Board, which was subsequently accepted, for a pilot project to test the feasibility of the concept. They agreed to pay the teaching half of the salary. The research salary was to be paid from special research grants, and the cost of the research (equipment, computer costs, and so on) would be borne by the university.

The purpose of the program is *not* to replace the present high school teachers with Ph.D. researchers, but rather to provide each high school with one teacher who is engaged in scientific research in physics, chemistry, mathematics, biology, and other fields. The benefits to the high school will be several. There is the stimulating effect of the direct personal classroom contact between the researcher and the high school students. Similarly, there is the contact between the researcher and the other high school teachers. The research teacher also may provide direct liaison with the university. For example, he could organize colloquia in the high school for students and staff involving various people from the university, including professors, post-doctoral fellows, and graduate students; and he could include students and high school colleagues in his research projects. Finally, the research teacher may serve as an important resource person. In addition to teaching one or two courses, the research teacher can spark discussions throughout the science program of the high school by joining other classes for short periods of time.

There is a basic premise that underlies this program. It is argued that because university professors engage in research, the quality of their teaching is better. I do not know if this is true in all cases, but it is widely recognized that the presence of researchers at the university enhances its teaching activity. At the same time, the university is frequently criticized, by its students and by others, for not paying sufficient attention to teaching techniques and methods. The benefits of having a research scientist participating in the high school program therefore would be reciprocal. The students and staff would benefit through contact with a person aware of recent scientific developments and actively engaged in research work of his own; and the research teachers would teach at university level at some time during their career and would be able to apply the experience and competence they would acquire in the high school context.

The major criticism that my scheme has elicited goes something like this: "Well, just because a person has a Ph.D. does not mean he or she will be a good teacher, especially in the high school." Of course not. On the other hand, possession of a Ph.D. does not mean that he or she will necessarily be a *bad* teacher either. To ensure that our research teachers will be able to relate well to high school students, they must be carefully screened, and no one should be accepted into the program without first being observed teaching a class of high school students. Those Ph.D.s who participate in the pilot scheme will have to take a full year at the college of education, in addition to their graduate studies, in order to be properly certified. If the project proves a success, it may be reasonable to study the possibilities of integrating graduate studies with high school teacher education at the college of education. Although it is unlikely that there will ever be many individuals involved in such a program, the development of a group of Ph.D.-level research scientists who devote part of their time to teaching in the high schools would have a very beneficial effect on the quality of education both in our secondary schools and in our universities.

PART THREE
Future Directions

Salvaging the Wreckage: Ontario 1971-1973

Douglas Myers

The Ontario misadventure in the reorganization of the teacher education system has continued to run true to form ever since negotiations between the provincial government and the universities were abruptly suspended in August 1971. At that time, the Minister of Education stated that a major review of the situation would be undertaken immediately. On the basis of this study, a new "master plan" would be drawn up to complete the government's policy of transferring teacher education to the universities. Department officials indicated that the plan would be released later that year.

In fact, two completely unrelated review studies of teacher education were undertaken in the autumn of 1971. In June, before the suspension of negotiations had been announced, the government appointed the Committee on the Costs of Education. This seven-member committee had a wide mandate to examine, evaluate, and make recommendations concerning all aspects of the costs of elementary and secondary school programs in the province. Although there was no specific mention of teacher education in its charge, the committee chose to make the investigation of the teacher education system its first priority.[1] It devoted several months to the subject, met with representatives from all the teacher education institutions in the province, and completed its report in February 1972.[2] At the same time, the Department of Education was proceeding with its own review study of the situation.

But no "master plan" announcement resulted from all this industry. Indeed the announcement of such a plan was to remain imminent for almost two years from the time of the original suspension of negotiations. The committee's *Interim Report, Number One* and its recommendations were kept under wraps, the Minister explaining that he was using it for background information. The Minister and his officials regularly promised that a master plan would be made public in the near future, but no announcements were forthcoming. The continuing atmosphere of anxiety, rumor, and confusion thus generated did nothing to improve morale in the remaining teachers' colleges, and in fact cast a general pall over teacher education in the province.

The reasons for this delay became apparent when, on May 25, 1973, the Minister of Education, Thomas Wells, finally tabled the *Interim Report, Number One* in the Ontario legislature and announced the next phase of the Ministry of Education's teacher education policy. The contrast between the report and the Minister's statement was marked and revealing. The former was brisk, clear cut, and to the point. Like Mr. Gradgrind, the committee dealt only with "facts" — with demographic, financial, and enrollment statistics. On the basis of the figures it had amassed, the committee predicted that Ontario's annual need for newly graduated elementary teachers would decline steadily through the 1970s, from a projected high point of 4,386 in 1972 to a low of 3,752 in 1978.[3] At the secondary level, the pattern would be somewhat different: the annual demand for new graduates would hold relatively steady between 2,400 and 2,700 until the end of the decade, when there would be a sudden decline to below 2,000.[4] The occult art of manpower forecasting, of course, is notoriously treacherous and uncertain. Only time and events will confirm or contradict the validity and accuracy of the committee's assumptions and projections.[5] On the basis of these statistics, however, the committee had little difficulty in reaching some unequivocal policy recommendations.

The committee concluded that, since there was already a marked oversupply of places available in training institutions at the elementary level, the number of places should be reduced by eliminating several of these institutions. Accordingly, it was recommended that four teachers' colleges — Stratford, Peterborough, Hamilton, and Ottawa — be closed outright. The remaining four — London, Toronto, Sudbury, and North Bay — should be amalgamated with the appropriate universities, as originally intended, without further delay. Since teacher education institutions for the secondary school level were operating at close to full capacity, and only a slight increase in facilities might be needed in future, the committee recommended further that most of the new university faculties of education limit themselves to elementary teacher training. Only York University, according to the committee, should expand its program at the secondary level. The committee also followed up these basic recommendations by urging the withdrawal of the Ministry from any involvement in part-time, continuing, in-service, or certification courses for teachers. The Teacher Education Branch, it felt, should be reduced to the status of a section in the Curriculum Branch.[6]

For the government and the Ministry of Education, however, things were not quite so simple. Mr. Wells's unenviable task was to rescue from the ruins of the Davis policy of 1966 a solution that would be, as far as possible, both economically viable and politically acceptable.[7] The integrations accomplished between 1966 and 1971, having proceeded on an ad hoc basis, had resulted in an incoherent overall pattern. This pattern had to be completed and rationalized. The Minister had to consider a whole range of economic, institutional, and political implications in each local situation. Each particular decision had to be set in the context of the province as a whole and weighed against the draconian measures urged by the Committee on Costs. All these considerations were evident in the Minister's lengthy statement on May 25, 1973. By no stretch of the imagination could that statement be described as a master plan. Though he did his best to represent the Ministry's actions as coherent, consistent, and deliberate, Mr. Wells in fact announced a series of particular decisions that, taken together, constituted a further, somewhat faltering, step toward completing the reorganization of Ontario teacher education, begun seven years before. The Committee on Costs had recommended that of the eight remaining teachers' colleges four be closed and four amalgamated as soon as possible. The Ministry announced the closure of two — Stratford and Peterborough — the amalgamation of three — London, Sudbury, and North Bay — and the continuation of three as teachers' colleges for at least one more year — Hamilton, Ottawa, and Toronto.

The decision to close Stratford was perhaps the easiest to reach. There was no university immediately adjacent, the logic of the move was widely accepted, and the college was small.[8] Peterborough, however, was more difficult. There was an articulate local concern that a teacher education facility be maintained in the area.[9] From the outset of the reorganization negotiations in the mid-1960s, Trent University in Peterborough had demonstrated an interest in setting up a teacher education program. More recently, in fact, Trent had taken initiatives, along with Queen's University in Kingston, to try to ensure that some type of regionally based teacher education program would be available. The government therefore accepted what on the surface seemed to be a curious double shuffle: the teachers' college was indeed to be closed and its staff moved to Kingston; its program, however, was to be replaced by a joint Queen's/Trent program to be offered at Trent University. As Mr. Wells put it, he was "pleased to say ... that officials of Trent University ... and Queen's University, have initiated discussions with a view to developing a co-operative programme of teacher education [to be offered in the Peterborough area]." Though still at a very early planning stage, the intention seems to be that Trent will offer a concurrent undergraduate program in arts, science, and education, and will arrange and supervise the practical experience in the schools; the students will attend Queen's for a term or two for courses on methodology.[10] Whether this arrangement will prove to be significantly more economical than two separate faculties is questionable. Nevertheless, it does recognize the regional political interests of the area and may prove to be a valuable example of inter-university cooperation.

The decision to amalgamate London Teachers' College with the University of Western Ontario was as predictable as the decision to close Stratford. An agreement to do so had been ready for signing in August 1971, and Althouse College, training secondary school teachers, was an established part of that university. The new faculty would serve a populous and important area.

Sudbury and North Bay represented somewhat more complicated situations. Economics and enrollment made a North Bay teacher education institution an especially doubtful proposition.[11] But the neglect of the midnorthern region of the province has been an increasingly potent issue in provincial politics in recent years. Moreover, the explosive tensions over education between the French- and English-speaking groups in that region made it imperative that both communities be adequately served in teacher preparation. A contributing factor in preserving teacher education in North Bay may have been the relocation of the teachers' college, in 1972, to a newly designed and built education center, along with three other local education institutions. This cooperative enterprise was locally initiated and strongly supported by the community. The withdrawal of any of the original participating institutions would have been deeply resented.

Most difficult of all were the circumstances surrounding the teachers' colleges in Hamilton, Ottawa, and Toronto. The Committee on Costs had recommended closing the first two and amalgamating the last with the University of Toronto. The Ministry declined to grasp these political nettles, however, and chose procrastination as the safest course. As the Minister phrased it: "Final decisions, Mr. Speaker, on the place within our overall teacher education programme of the teachers' colleges in Hamilton, Ottawa and Toronto, will be made at a later date based on our continuing analysis and review of all matters pertaining to teacher education in Ontario."[12]

In Hamilton, the problem was St. Catharines: an agreement had been concluded in 1971 to transfer St. Catharines Teachers' College to Brock

University, but no such agreement had been reached regarding the transfer of Hamilton Teachers' College to McMaster University. In a sense, success had been achieved at the wrong place. The result was, as the Committee on Costs pointed out, the existence of two teacher education institutions "so close together [that is, 35 miles] that the continued operation of both means that neither institution is any longer a viable operation for teacher education."[13] The committee recommended the closing of the larger and longer established of the two because of the economics of the situation and the fact that little progress had been made toward concluding an agreement with McMaster. Moreover, in St. Catharines, "a full utilization of facilities in the College of Education will contribute to the viability of Brock University itself."[14] Presumably, McMaster University would survive with or without teacher education.

The Minister's dilemma was plain. Whatever the economics of the situation, the inhabitants of Hamilton were unlikely to acquiesce passively in the disappearance of an old, established civic institution or to welcome the news that prospective teachers in their area must trek to St. Catharines or Toronto for training.[15] On the other hand, dismantling the agreement at Brock would have serious consequences for the viability of that university and would therefore be equally unpalatable. So Mr. Wells stalled. It seems unlikely, however, that the government will be able to entirely do away with a teacher education facility in Hamilton.

A somewhat similar dilemma faced the Ministry with regard to Ottawa, but in this case the problem was complicated by language considerations. With an expanded elementary teacher education program at Queen's University in Kingston, which already provided secondary school teacher education for the entire eastern region of the province, and with declining enrollment, it did not seem feasible to the Committee on the Costs of Education to maintain a second facility in an aging, though handsome, building in Ottawa.[16] No agreement had been reached with Ottawa's Carleton University, nor did it seem appropriate to transfer English-speaking teacher education into the primarily French-speaking faculty of education at the University of Ottawa. But the Ministry faced obvious political dangers in closing the teachers' college and making Queen's responsible for all English-speaking teacher education in eastern Ontario. The language problem is a highly visible and sensitive issue, at both the federal and provincial levels, in the capital and the Ottawa Valley. In the question period immediately following his announcement in May, for example, Mr. Wells was forced to deny that he was attempting "to deprive anyone in the Ottawa Valley of English-language teacher education,"[17] even though a decision to close Ottawa Teachers' College would certainly be interpreted that way by a sizable group in the area.

Moreover, having acknowledged the regional interests of the Trent Valley, the government will find it difficult to ignore similar considerations in the Ottawa Valley. Again, a cooperative Carleton/Queen's arrangement may be the best solution, and may be what the government will attempt to promote.

Finally, the Ministry also postponed action on Toronto Teachers' College. One may surmise that the Ministry found the prospect of integrating the province's two largest teacher education institutions — the Toronto Teachers' College and the Faculty of Education at the University of Toronto[18] — at least as daunting as the closing of the colleges in Hamilton and Ottawa. Relations between the Ministry and the University of Toronto concerning teacher education have always been difficult. The University has been conducting its own review of its internal relations with its faculty of education and with OISE, and this would be further complicated by the addition of a teachers' college located five miles from the main campus.

In addition, for some time there has been a strong view, emanating from a number of officials in the Ministry's Teacher Education Branch, that some alternative to amalgamating the University and Toronto Teachers' College may be desirable. Total transfer of teacher education to the universities, so the argument runs, is obviously not an unmixed blessing. It might be beneficial, therefore, to have a teacher education institution outside this pattern, either directly supervised by the Ministry or established as an independent, non-university institution. Although such an arrangement would involve considerable organizational difficulties, it is clearly an idea worth serious attention. It would make no sense, for example, for such an institution to be restricted to elementary teacher education, as Toronto Teachers' College is at present. So far, however, there has been no hint that the Ministry is prepared to consider any exception to the standard pattern. At the moment, it must be assumed that the Ministry intends to try to work out an agreement on the amalgamation of Toronto Teachers' College with the University of Toronto.

Where do we go from here? The agonies of reorganization will have lasted almost a decade by the time the integration process is completed. What difference will it all have made? Will the same old business merely be conducted by different proprietors? Will teacher education occupy an obscure corner of the groves of academe, downgraded by the government ministries, barely tolerated by the universities, and ignored by the teachers? At present, these seem the most likely possibilities.

If anything of positive significance is to emerge from the present situation, the main parties involved — the ministries, the universities and faculties, and the teachers — have to make some fresh commitments and set some new priorities. This will not be easy, because no single institution or group has the authority or power to impose its will on the others. The government, having handed over responsibility to the universities, is in no position to demand or require adherence to the policies it favors. Nor would it be desirable that it should have such unilateral power. At the same time, if university autonomy is used primarily as a justification for continued institutional rivalry and completely uncoordinated development, teacher education will be served no better. Teachers in the field lack the entrenched power of either the government or the universities. Nevertheless, if they were sufficiently concerned, political, and energetic, they could exert a very significant and constructive influence on the qualifications and training of those who will enter their profession.

The reorganization shambles demonstrates above all that the very real differences of attitude and interest that exist among those involved in teacher education cannot be evaded or glossed over. Those differences must be recognized, fundamental issues identified, and a number of province-wide guidelines and priorities worked out. This can be done only on a voluntary and cooperative basis.

A basic problem is the lack of a generally acceptable forum in which all the parties concerned can discuss and resolve the central issues in Ontario teacher education. The Department of Education, as noted previously, did not implement the MacLeod Committee's recommendation to set up a representative provincial committee to oversee and advise upon the integration process. The Ministry remains reluctant to establish any advisory body of this sort. A hopeful indication of a willingness to take an independent initiative in this direction was provided by the deans of education and the Ontario Teachers' Federation, who, in April 1973, cosponsored a two-day invitational conference in Toronto to discuss the problems of teacher involvement in teacher education and of continuing education for teachers. At this meeting, an ad hoc teacher education liaison committee was formed, representing the faculties, teachers' colleges, and teachers' organizations. It may be that a more substantial and more widely representative advisory body might be developed on this base, to consider issues of common concern.[19]

Assuming that some mutually acceptable forum can be established in which continuing discussion and consultation can take place, there seem to be three major problems deserving urgent attention. The first is financial. In this period of retrenchment in educational spending, it is essential to ensure that teacher education receives an adequate supply of funds to enable it to take new and more imaginative directions. The experience of the 1960s provides convincing evidence that huge expenditures on buildings, technology, and prepackaged curricula will not significantly improve the quality of education: the teacher remains the key factor. The fact that the pressure is now off the training institutions to produce ever-increasing masses of teachers to fill new classrooms should provide an opportunity to reexamine and reshape the goals and programs of teacher education. That opportunity may well be lost unless the government provides adequate funding for experimentation and development as well as for maintenance, unless the universities give teacher education at least the status and the level of support they accord other professional schools on campus, and unless teachers themselves recognize the importance of teacher education in terms of improving their own teaching, their professional position, and their conditions of work.[20]

The second problem concerns the definition of teacher education itself. As other articles in this collection point out (see, for example, the contributions by Gidney, Linden, and Milburn, and by Ready), there is a notable lack of financial support, recognition, and comprehensive provision for professional education opportunities for practicing teachers. Most of the emphasis in Ontario is given to pre-service teacher education and, more recently, to graduate studies in education. With the establishment of the new faculties of education, there is a very real danger that the universities will tend to expand facilities for graduate studies rather than move into the continuing education field. It is clear that any preservice program is necessarily limited in its relevance and effectiveness by the inexperience of its candidates. But it is equally clear that graduate studies are not an appropriate avenue of further education for more than a minority of teachers. Again, the time is opportune, with the decline in enrollment and the oversupply of new faculties, to make a major shift into continuing education. Such a development would have a significant effect on improving the quality of education in this province. Here again, measures to provide adequate financial and organizational support must be worked out by the government, the universities and their faculties, the boards of education, and the teachers.

Finally, some balance must be struck between general provincial standards and guidelines and particular regional or institutional diversity. Unless this problem is addressed directly, all of the new faculties may end up looking very much the same and offering a very similar type of program. Above all, teacher education needs some diversity and imaginative specialization. There is no evidence to suggest that there is a single "right" or "best" way to educate and train teachers. As Duthie suggests in the article that follows, what we need is to encourage, develop, and compare some coherent and systematic alternative approaches. To achieve this will require an unprecedented degree of candor, cooperation, and commitment from the parties involved.

It may be that the disillusioning ordeal of reorganization has taken too high a toll, that the challenge of making fresh commitments and developing new priorities may be too daunting to be faced by those institutions and groups. If so, the government's teacher education reorganization policy will stand as one of the most dismal failures in education in the history of this province. But if the challenge can be met, the reorganization will have been merely an unfortunate and tedious prelude to the genuine reform of teacher education in Ontario.

NOTES

1. According to Thomas Wells, Robert Welch's successor as Minister of Education, the committee was not specifically asked to do so by the Department. "I had no idea to what the Committee on Costs of Education were going to direct themselves in the first instance," he told the legislature in 1973. "Their first interim report dealt with teacher education, which we were studying in an ongoing manner in the ministry." Ontario, Legislative Assembly, *Debates*, 29th Leg., 3rd Session, May 25, 1973, p. 2277.
2. Committee on the Costs of Education, T. A. McEwan, chairman, *Interim Report, Number One: Report on the Education of Elementary and Secondary Teachers in Ontario: Facilities, Organization, Administration* (Toronto: Ontario Department of Education, dated February 1972; released in May 1973), referred to hereafter as *Interim Report, Number One*.
3. Ibid., table 2, p. 29. The committee projected a decline in elementary school enrollment from its all-time high of about 1,500,000 students in 1970 to 1,300,000 by 1980, and a corresponding decline in the total number of elementary teachers from about 59,000 to 51,000.
4. Ibid., table 4, p. 31. These figures were based on a continued gradual increase in the number of students at the secondary level from about 600,000 in 1972 to a high of 650,000 in 1977, with a similar gradual decline thereafter. The corresponding figures for total secondary school teachers were a high of 38,700 in 1977, up from 35,000 in 1972.
5. One assumption, in particular, is worth noting. On the crucial and controversial question of teacher–pupil ratios, the committee operated on the assumption that they would "not be less" than their 1971 levels — that is, 1:24.9 in the elementary schools and 1:16.6 in the secondary schools (ibid., pp. 7–9).
6. Ibid., pp. 63–87.
7. It is interesting to note that the Secretary to the Committee on the Costs of Education was Dr. J. R. McCarthy, Deputy Minister of Education under William Davis during the original attempts to implement the 1966 teacher education policy.

8. It had an enrollment of 182 in 1971, the fourth lowest of all the teachers' colleges in the province, down from 345 in 1970.

9. The successful Conservative candidate in the 1971 provincial election, John N. Turner, had made the preservation of Peterborough Teachers' College one of the main issues in his campaign. The previous M.P.P., Walter Pitman (NDP), had been on record for several years as being in favor of a Trent Valley teacher education program.

10. *Debates*, May 25, 1973, p. 2276.

11. In 1971, North Bay Teachers' College had an enrollment of 170, the third lowest in the province, down from 392 the previous year.

12. *Debates*, May 25, 1973, p. 2276.

13. *Interim Report, Number One*, p. 71. The report states that in 1971 Hamilton Teachers' College had a capacity of 720 students and an enrollment of 439. The College of Education at Brock had a capacity of 430 and an actual enrollment of 118. The combined capacity of both was stated as 1,150, with an actual enrollment of 548 (possibly this last figure should read 557).

14. Ibid., p. 71.

15. Civic pride is a notable feature of Hamilton life — for example, the city's new buses are painted in the colors of its football team. In the spring of 1973, the Mayor of Hamilton was ejected from the public gallery at Queen's Park for attempting to put his city's point of view regarding regional government proposals to the members of the legislature.

16. The building was opened in 1875. In 1971, its enrollment was 311, down from 840 in 1970.

17. *Debates*, May 25, 1973, p. 2278.

18. In 1971, Toronto Teachers' College had a capacity of 1,200 students and an enrollment of 1,263, down from 1,857 in 1970. The Faculty of Education at Toronto had a capacity of 1,500 and an enrollment of 1,455, down from 1,475 the year before. Their combined enrollment accounted for over 35 percent of the provincial total.

19. See "OTF/Deans' Conference on Teacher Education in Ontario," mimeographed report (Toronto: Ontario Teachers' Federation, 1973).

20. There is some indication that the teachers' organizations are moving in this direction. OTF, as a result of its concern about the difficulties of reorganization, has devoted a good deal of effort over the past couple of years to becoming better informed about the situation, developing strategies and policies to achieve more effective involvement with the teacher education institutions, and supporting teachers in exerting a positive influence on the faculties in their area. (See *An Action Guide to Teacher Education in Ontario* [Toronto: Ontario Teachers' Federation, 1973].) It remains to be seen whether the OTF and its five affiliate bodies will make the long-range commitment of resources and personnel necessary to enable teachers to make a significant, constructive contribution to improving teacher education.

Research and Innovation in Teacher Education

J. H. Duthie

The difficulties encountered in implementing the MacLeod Report in Ontario illustrate two basic problems in educational reform and reorganization. On the one hand, the recommendations of such reports are often ignored entirely or implemented in such a piecemeal fashion as to be only incidentally connected with their source. On the other hand, major policies are sometimes initiated on the basis of such reports. This is equally unfortunate, as events following from the MacLeod Report have shown, because recommendations for action of this sort, based merely on the deliberations of a committee, may be inappropriate, not to say misguided and dangerous.

This is not to deny the need for an examination of the educational requirements of society and a statement of objectives. But these are not enough. A report on education should be only the first stage in a long process. The conclusions of a report should as far as possible be stated in the form of alternative strategies, and these should then be evaluated by a program of research. The results of this research should make it possible to reach decisions about the most appropriate ways of achieving the objectives originally set (this might involve matching different strategies to specific circumstances and to economic conditions). Only in this way will it be possible for a committee to know whether the recommendations it makes are viable.

Had the MacLeod recommendations regarding the takeover of teacher education by the universities been tested against other forms of organization both within and without the universities, we would now (seven years later) be in a much better position to know whether or not these recommendations were sensible. Education reform, then, might proceed in two stages. The first stage would be the investigations and deliberations of an appointed committee, which would produce a series of recommendations or hypotheses for teacher education.[1] The second stage would involve the implementation of these recommendations on an experimental or pilot-project basis, with careful attention to evaluation and assessment. This second stage might well be conducted and monitored under the auspices of a provincial standing committee representing all educational interests, particularly those of teachers.

This model ignores the distinction between "pure" research and "developmental" research (in the case of educational research, the distinction is probably less clear than elsewhere). To relate the two, the standing committee would have both "pure" and "developmental" research subcommittees. Pure research would be commissioned by the standing committee on a similar basis to the commissioning of developmental projects. This arrangement would provide a raison d'être for pure research and might also give it some direction, which at present seems to be lacking.

The day-to-day business and responsibilities of the standing committee could be handled by a secretariat, and annual or semiannual provincial conferences could consider long-range issues and problems. Although this structure may appear to be monolithic, in the Ontario context this could be easily avoided. Government representation could provide adequate public control, and other institutions and parties could be cooperatively and voluntarily involved in the policies and direction of the standing committee in order to maintain diversity and flexibility. Such a structure could do much to ensure the relevance of research (that is, to produce research that is likely to be implemented, in contrast to the majority of present research projects, which founder because no one listens), to encourage the coordination of research efforts, and, it is hoped, to help government policy makers to base their decisions on firmer foundations.

In any case, the general principle remains, however it is realized: a temporary committee making recommendations that can only be blindly implemented or rejected is to be deplored (this applies to the James Committee in England as well as to the MacLeod Committee in Canada). An alternative that is both permanent and flexible is necessary.

The membership of an Ontario standing committee on teacher education would include teachers, teachers' federation representatives, university and faculty of education staff, OISE staff, government department representatives, directors of education, and project directors. In addition each subcommittee would have a consultant on research design although one consultant might serve on both subcommittees.

All project directors would be full voting members of the standing committee, not simply observers. They would not be expected to attend all meetings (although they could do so if they wished) — only those relevant to their research. The chairman of the standing committee would be responsible for directing the attention of project directors to relevant meetings. The size of the committee should be restricted to about twenty working members at any one time.

The standing committee would commission the initial project independently, or on the suggestion of a project director, or — most likely — on the basis of the findings of a previous study. It would also monitor ongoing projects.

The project director would be responsible for discussing with the committee the appropriateness of his research to the objectives set, for proposing a research design and strategy (in consultation with the standing committee consultant), and for presenting progress reports to the committee. It would be important for the project director to be a full voting member of the committee and for him to be given freedom to carry out the research between reports. He would also be free to write the final report, although for political reasons he would be wise to accept the advice of members of the committee as to the most appropriate way to frame results and recommendations.

A special word might be added here about the possible role of the Ontario Institute for Studies in Education in this context. The Institute might well provide a base or support system for the proposed structure. This would both utilize the considerable resources of the Institute, including the talents of its staff, and help to bridge the gulf between isolated education research and its implementation. The continuing efforts of OISE to relate its research and development projects more closely to the field seem to indicate a move in this direction.

Although committees are not necessarily the ideal medium for educational reform, the plethora of uncoordinated and, at best, unimplemented research indicates the need for some structure to coordinate the research effort and ensure its relevance. I do not know of the existence of any fully realized structure of this kind, but I have had the experience of directing research for two years on a project on the use of auxiliary helpers (such as teacher aides and paraprofessionals) in Scottish primary schools, which presented a microcosm of the model outlined here.[2] The project consisted of a research team of five, working with a consultative committee of twenty-two that had a membership similar to that described above. The structure, then, was rather like a single strand of the model that is proposed here, with the difference that it related to only one project.

At the time the project was set up, the idea of using auxiliaries in primary schools was political dynamite. The fact that the idea is now nationally accepted and that auxiliaries are now employed in schools on an experimental basis is, I believe, due to our being able to carry political opinion with us through every step of the experiment. It was, of course, much harder to carry out the research under these circumstances than it would have been to do so without strings; but had we taken the latter course of action, I am certain that we would have failed to get our proposals implemented.

One other Scottish development points in the same direction. In 1965 a consultative committee on the curriculum was set up by the Secretary of State for Scotland. There are twenty-four members on the committee, including teachers, university and college faculty, directors of education, and school inspectors. The chairman is the Secretary of the Scottish Education Department.

The first report of the committee contains the following statement of policy:

> The Committee does not itself examine detailed problems, but identifies aspects of the curriculum which it considers should be further investigated. It may recommend to the Secretary of State how these enquiries should be carried out, whether by *ad hoc* working parties or sub-committees.[3]

A number of objections to such a proposal are likely to be raised. It might seem that it would restrict unduly the freedom of the research worker. This is a relatively small price to pay for the assurance that one's research, if developmental, is seriously considered and likely to be implemented by those in a position to do so — and, if pure, is likely to be relevant and to contribute to the solution of current problems, whether they be theoretical or practical. The strongest objections to this thesis would come from the pure researcher. I would refer him to an article by J. G. Taylor, who described the scene on his side of the Atlantic:[4] my recent time in Canada does not lead me to think the position is very different here. Taylor's article suggests that most pure research is vapid, designed to prove to the world (and to future employers) how rigorous and elegant the author is. If there is any truth in this statement, then perhaps the discipline imposed by working within a structure such as the one I have suggested would improve matters, at least in the field of education. It might also help to alleviate one of the problems that faces the research worker in education and psychology, the lack of a theoretical framework to provide cohesion and a sense of direction.[5]

What are the alternatives if the research worker wants to disseminate his research results? He may publish; but the average readership for journals has been shown to be very small indeed. This is not surprising, in view of the immense number of articles published in journals every year — a problem that affects the physical as well as the social sciences.[6] There seems to be little hope that such sources would be read by those who are responsible for implementing research results. An alternative must be found if we are to make progress. This is not to say that journals would atrophy if this plan were adopted. International communication of research results would remain vital. But journals would no longer be the sole, or indeed the prime, means of communication between researcher and implementer. Rather, these individuals would consult each other and discuss the research long before it got off the ground. (As a subsidiary benefit, one would hope that the number of journals and journal articles would diminish and that those that were published would be worth reading.)

One other possible objection is that the freedom of the teacher might be threatened by committees as powerful as those I have described. This need not be so. To quote again from the Consultative Committee on the Curriculum's *First Report*:

> While the Committee provides advice to the Secretary of State which he may publish and commend to education authorities and teachers, neither the Secretary of State nor the Scottish Education Department has any direct responsibility for the school curriculum. Education authorities . . . acting with the advice of the heads of their schools and their teachers decide what shall, or shall not, be taught in their schools (subject to the statutory requirements for the provision of instruction in religion) and it is for them to decide whether or not to accept any advice which is offered to them.[7]

Leslie Hunter, however, states that

> while this is true in theory, in practice considerable pressures operate to give force to the advice. . . . Thus the Papers, Reports, and Memoranda published on the advice of the Consultative Committee, although they are not Departmental directives, are clear indicators of central policy; and Inspectors certainly use them for guidance in the field.[8]

The degree of control over the activities of the classroom teacher would be a matter for local decision — in Scotland, at any rate. According to Hunter,

> There is evidence to show that very many teachers, far from resenting Departmental initiative, appreciate being given clear guide lines from the central authority. It tends to be assumed that the Department knows best, and thus its views are generally accepted.[9]

The proposal contained in this paper, then, need not be perceived by teachers as a threat, particularly if they themselves are strongly represented in the committees and, it is hoped, in the research projects as well.

Both in this article and in my description of the concurrent program at Stirling University earlier in this book, I have tried to make a case for careful, rather small-scale testing of proposals for new approaches to teacher education. If educational reports of the MacLeod type are to continue — and one article, no matter how well argued, is unlikely to change affairs in this respect — then they should take the form of proposals for research rather than recommendations for action. But an educational report is too much of a cut-and-dried affair. What is required is a strategy that ties research to innovation and permits innovation to be evaluated and modified accordingly.

I have proposed that an appropriate context for such a research strategy is one in which a standing committee consisting of all interested parties — teachers, politicians, academics, and researchers — initiates and monitors research carried out by ad hoc research teams. Such a context will help to ensure that, in future, research in teacher education in Ontario is coherent, relevant, and, above all, implemented.

NOTES

1. Of course, there would be sources for such proposals and hypotheses other than official committees.

2. J. H. Duthie, *Primary School Survey: A Study of the Teacher's Day* (Edinburgh: H.M.S.O., 1970).

3. Scottish Education Department, Consultative Committee on the Curriculum, *First Report, 1965/8* (Edinburgh: H.M.S.O., 1969).

4. "Experimental Design: A Cloak for Intellectual Sterility," *British Journal of Psychology* 49 (1958): 106–116.

5. This point of view is reinforced by Michael Young in his book *Innovation and Research in Education* (London: Routledge & Kegan Paul, 1965). He argues that the researcher and innovator should be inseparable; one cannot function effectively without the other.

6. See, for example, P. Earle and B. Vickery, "Social Science Literature Use in the U.K. as Indicated by Citations," *Journal of Documentation* 25, no. 2 (1969): 123–41; D. N. Wood and C. A. Bower, "The Use of Social Science Periodical Literature," *Journal of Documentation* 25, no. 2 (1969): 108–22; A. Herschman, "The Primary Journal: Past, Present, and Future," *Journal of Chemical Documentation* 10, no. 1 (February 1970): 37–42; and G. London, "The Publication Inflation," *American Documentation* 19, no. 2 (1968): 137–41.

7. Scottish Education Department, *First Report, 1965/8*.

8. S. L. Hunter, *The Scottish Educational System*, 2d ed. (Oxford and Toronto: Pergamon Press, 1972), p. 38.

9. Ibid., p. 38.

Teachers and Teaching Competencies

John A. Tickle

Those charged with the task of revising Ontario's teacher education programs, beware! Many authorities would have you believe that a traditional general arts degree for elementary teachers is the panacea for all the past and future problems of education. Many reports recommend the extension of conservative programs already traditional to secondary school teacher education to elementary teacher education: a three-year academic program concurrent with or consecutive to one year of teacher training. This was proposed by the 1966 MacLeod Report, which at this point in time seems to have made the greatest impact on teacher education in Ontario. Those who wish to make a positive contribution to teacher education in the future should reassess the recommendations of that report.

The MacLeod Report states:

> It is evident that there are fundamental weaknesses in teacher education in Ontario which cannot be resolved under the present system. It appears that the major deficiencies are related to inadequate academic education and insufficient maturity on the part of the student teacher.[1]

This empirical statement is offered as the major premise of the Report's rationale for the majority of the recommendations that follow. But it begs several basic questions. What are the "fundamental weaknesses" it mentions? And what evidence supports the conclusion that academic education and maturity will eliminate these weaknesses? The contention that extended academic education and time to mature will improve elementary teacher education implies that secondary school teachers are *more* effective teachers than their colleagues in the elementary schools. Nonsense! The illogic continues with the assumption that academic education and maturity can be achieved only "within the university milieu." This statement implies that anyone without a university degree is in some way intellectually and emotionally inferior to one who holds one. The recent history of our universities, however, must raise serious doubts that these institutions can lay confident claim to the exclusive right to provide education and training for any particular profession.

At all levels of education, the paramount concern of educators today should be the search for reasonable *alternatives*. What alternatives did the MacLeod Committee explore? A university setting *may* be the best alternative to a teachers' college; but if competence in the art of teaching is one criterion for successful teacher education, it is reasonable to suggest that there is no significant correlation between academic standing and teaching effectiveness in many educational institutions. If the problem is that teacher education is inadequate, then the first step should be to identify the factors affecting adequate preparation of teachers. If academic education and maturity are the only factors affecting the competence of teachers (which is doubtful), the identification of the variables affecting academic growth and maturation might suggest some reasonable alternatives to the present system. In fact, the only alternative suggested by the committee that may reasonably improve teacher education is the extension of the training period to four years.

The MacLeod Committee seemed to believe that the move into the universities would improve the professional status of elementary school teachers in Ontario. Public opinion in this respect is not limited to elementary teachers; it applies to teachers generally, and with reason: that the teachers of Ontario — elementary, secondary, or university — should call themselves professionals when most have received no more than one year of professional training, and some none at all, is ludicrous.

The two main criteria that society applies to professionalism are the period of professional training and proven competence. Count the number of recognized professions in Ontario that require a maximum of one year's training and do not control the certification of their members. If teachers want to be professionals, they must extend the professional training period and establish some acceptable standard of competence. One can only conclude that the committee believed professionalism is measured by "letters," because its recommended "professional" training program required the same one-year period that has operated since 1904.[2]

Although the committee seemed to recognize that competence in teaching would not necessarily be achieved by increasing a teacher's knowledge of the content of a discipline,[3] it still overemphasized the liberal arts aspect of teacher education. Moreover, it failed to suggest any reasonable alternatives, even in terms of the professional training aspect of the process. For example, the report recommends that the practice-teaching component of professional training be allocated a total of twelve weeks in the final year of the four-year program. Splendid! But this "recommendation" has been a fact in teacher education in Ontario since the early 1960s.

Perhaps the basic problem with the MacLeod Report is that it seemed to get the priorities wrong. Teacher education should be defined, first, in relation to what teachers should do for children, and second, in terms of what it should do for the teacher as an individual. Consequently, the focus of teacher education should be to devise a program that is consistent with the express purpose of developing competencies in the art of teaching.

Fundamental Competencies
The purpose of teacher education is to prepare prospective teachers to intervene in the intellectual, emotional, and physical development of children. Successful intervention seems to depend upon a number of fundamental competencies, and these competencies should be the basis for the professional training program of teachers.

The teacher's first competency must be a mature notion of *growth*; that is, the teacher should have conceptualized the dimensions in which the child may be expected to grow under the school's guidance, and the sequence of stages through which the child spontaneously passes in each dimension of growth. It is fashionable today to encourage the teacher to "let the child grow in his own way," to simply observe him and determine from his expressed needs the kinds of experience to which he should next be exposed. Although the rhetoric is appealing, the sobering fact is that no teacher provides experiences for a child on an entirely random basis. Behind the teacher's encouragement, prodding, or subtle redirecting, there is some notion of what the child's next stage of development should be, of the direction in which we hope he will move.

In our schools today, the teacher's efforts to promote growth lack potency because the teachers do not possess this conception. We cannot blame them for this. In the first place, they have normally observed children of a limited range of ages. Also, the need for a teacher to manage large groups has ruled out the possibility of long-term study of the individual child. A radically different approach is required for the teaching of child development, which traditionally has been a crude amalgam of the "omnibus approach" with specious bits of normative cross-sectional data. A course of instruction should be substituted that is akin to the developmental–observational work of Piaget, but related directly to the kinds of intellectual tasks that can be nurtured in the school environment. Certainly, the child's developing conceptions of numbers and space are important, but so are the abilities to question, to generate ideas, to plan, to judge the relevance of data, to synthesize information, to draw conclusions, and to generalize. Each of these skills defines a continuum of growth that the school wishes to nurture, but that has not been conceptualized by the vast majority of today's teachers and so cannot provide a basis for teacher intervention.

Once the teacher has conceptualized a dimension of growth, and hence presumably is able to determine the position of a particular child on that dimension, he or she can undertake the more arduous and demanding task of planning experiences that will encourage the child to grow to a more mature stage. It is with this second competency that the real art or science of pedagogy begins, and it seems a safe assumption that the more ingenious the pedagogy, the more rapid the child's growth. Of course, teachers vary greatly in terms of their pedagogic ingenuity, but we have no reason to believe that the average performance is high. Most potential teachers know what teachers do, but not what teachers *should* do. Again, it is a question of opportunity; for this kind of inventiveness depends, among other things, on their having time to plan and try out a variety of approaches on small groups of children besides meeting normal expectations and requirements. Teachers usually do not have this opportunity in their teacher training programs, and they certainly do not get it in the classroom.

The third prerequisite for successful intervention is that the teachers devote their energy to tasks that are critical for them to perform and turn over to other willing hands those that require a lower level of professional sophistication. Traditionally, the elementary school teacher has been regarded as a jack-of-all-trades who not only plans and teaches lessons in a variety of subjects, but is saddled with all the chores of materials preparation, secretarial work, and housekeeping as well. One consequence of this approach is that the teacher is more or less forced to work with large instructional groups and so has no time for intensive interaction with individual children. The second consequence is that the teacher's critical functions — those in which his personal, individual attention could make an enormous difference in the child's learning — have not become the center of his professional career; instead, the teacher is swamped by a welter of details. The expertise that has been developed by excellent teachers has evolved through trial-and-error experiences under adverse conditions.

The idea that the teacher should concentrate on critical teaching functions has become a reality in some schools as a result of the massive influx of both parents and other volunteers into our classrooms and the increased use by teachers of programmed materials. Accompanying this has been an attempt to clarify the crude distinctions between teaching and non-teaching roles. Typical of these efforts is the taxonomy prepared by Robinson and his colleagues, which describes the following major categories of activities intended to further the child's learning in school:

1. Planning: *a*) broad; *b*) narrow.
2. Motivation: *a*) broad; *b*) specific.
3. Instruction Sequence: *a*) initiating a concept, attitude, or skill; *b*) consolidating a new concept, attitude, or skill; *c*) adding content to structure; *d*) consolidating content.
4. Supervision: *a*) active; *b*) passive.
5. Technical Assistance: *a*) skilled; *b*) nonskilled.
6. Nontechnical Assistance.
7. Evaluation: *a*) designing of instruments; *b*) administration of tests; *c*) objective marking; *d*) subjective marking; *e*) interpretation of marking; *f*) diagnosis.[4]

In this conception, the teacher's professional role centers on long-range planning (which depends on a conception of growth) and getting the child to grasp those concepts or skills that constitute a further stage of development along some particular continuum. Once the child has grasped this concept, all the subsequent attempts to strengthen it, practice it, and make it automatic can be turned over to some other person or learning device. For instance, the child's grasp of the notion of addition (of joining sets together and counting the resulting group) constitutes a major step upward in his development along an "arithmetic" continuum. But once this notion is grasped, the child can use it to discover the addition facts himself. Thus, the entire task of adding detail to the concept, of practicing and consolidating it, can be handled by someone who does not have the competence to teach it initially. (Almost anyone, for example, can conduct a consolidation drill with flash cards.) Teacher specialization based upon the exercise of critical skills is no pie-in-the-sky proposal. Pilot classes have already been established in the Niagara region, where teachers work individually with children and are responsible for planning and initiating new concepts while lay volunteers — mostly mothers — assume all the other responsibilities.

A Proposed Teacher Training Program
It is safe to assume that adults of the future will still have a need to communicate. Therefore, the reading, writing, listening, and speaking skills of communication should be developed in future curricula. To predict the retention of any other traditional subjects on the school curriculum, with the exception of the arts, would be risky. This is not to say that knowledge that has been classified as historical, geographical,

scientific, or mathematical will be ignored; rather, the emphasis will be on the *use* of the knowledge as it applies to thinking and solving real problems, regardless of the discipline. If this premise and the rationale for teacher education previously outlined are accepted, it should be possible to design a viable teacher training program.

To develop teacher training programs that prepare teachers to conceptualize a growth pattern in the communication dimension, to identify the specific skills inherent in the various strands of communicating, and to identify the point at which a child may be functioning is not an insurmountable task. Some crude approximations of learning strands in communications are the basis of reading programs at many levels now being used throughout this province and others.

However, to develop teacher training programs that prepare teachers to intervene in the child's problem-solving growth is a real challenge. The place of rational thinking as a dimension of the school curriculum has received limited attention in the elementary school. Outside the schools, the notion that the development of rational thinking is a worthwhile goal of public education is under attack. I offer the following thoughts in support of my argument for this component of education.

The survival of man in a futuristic environment, with its demands for rapid change, will depend in great measure upon his ability to think and behave rationally. Schools today are beginning to respond to student demands and to the pressures of society that urge the discard of measures adopted at the turn of the century to prepare students for an industrialized society. Students are far more militant now than they were then in pursuing rational answers to age-old questions relating to curriculum, school organization, authority, and the value system of the school. At all levels of education, institutions are being criticized for their lack of relevance to the real world. Society in general and young people in particular have expressed their impatience with gradual change, and some have used methods to accelerate change that have been described as irresponsible, emotional, or destructive. I would suggest, however, that most educational institutions have failed to provide opportunities for children and young adults to learn what rational thinking is and how to apply it to problem solving.

If the development of rational thinking in school children is accepted as a major dimension of the curriculum, then one component of teacher preparation will be a course that addresses itself exclusively to rationality; not the traditional educational philosophy course, but one that recognizes the practical implications of rationality for the school curriculum. Teachers should have some precise conception of rational thinking. Through the study of the history of rational thinking and its role, teachers would gain insights into the growth patterns that need to be developed through future curricula. If teachers were given a foundation through this type of philosophy course, they would be able to defend with logic the position of the school against critics of the notion that rational thinking is a worthwhile goal of public education.

The development of rational thinking through school programs is the purpose of a project that has been under way since 1970 in the Port Colborne schools, in cooperation with the Niagara Centre of OISE. There is significant evidence that teachers can intervene in the learning of mental processes — in this case those involved in the logical thinking of grade 7 pupils. Studies are continuing in respect to the growth patterns of such learning strands as questioning, generating ideas, planning, judging the relevance of data, synthesizing information, drawing conclusions, and generalizing — continuums of skills referred to previously.

The discussion here has deliberately been limited to a two-dimensional elementary school curriculum: communications and problem solving. This approach does not exclude a range of other interests and themes, such as the development of value systems and moral judgment in children. In fact, the concomitant nature of problem solving and value conflict would *enhance* the child's chances of developing moral judgment. This approach is reflected in the recommendations of the Mackay Report in 1969:

> Although the recommended program is one which not every teacher will be able to implement easily, it assumes the active participation of every teacher, at every level from kindergarten to the end of grade 13. Because it is integrated with all the subjects of the curriculum through incidental teaching, it precludes the idea of separate classes in moral education, and it precludes the thought that only some teachers will be responsible for administering it.[5]

Improving Competencies

The position taken in this paper is that the objective of teacher education programs should be to assist prospective teachers in developing the competencies that they require to intervene successfully in the intellectual, emotional, and physical development of children. This position has a number of specific implications both for teacher education programs and for the school curriculum, particularly at the elementary level.

If teacher education institutions are to meet the objectives stated above, they must —
1. develop teacher training programs that attend to the defined skills, attitudes, and experiences required of individuals living and learning in the future;

2. require student teachers to behave as they will expect their students to behave, though at a level of greater sophistication;
3. subordinate content objectives to behavioral objectives;
4. accommodate the individual differences of potential teachers in the same way the graduate teacher will be expected to accommodate the individual differences of children;
5. require teachers to demonstrate a minimum level of competence in a range of critical functions in order to obtain professional certification.

Similarly, if teacher education programs are to have any relevance to what actually occurs in the schools, the schools themselves must —

1. provide programs based on a continuum of skills and concepts inherent in specific learning themes rather than in isolated subject matter;
2. adopt a philosophy of continuous progress;
3. provide opportunities within the school for the child to apply rational thinking to real-life problems;
4. actively implement new resources and techniques designed to relieve the teacher of non-teaching functions.

NOTES

1. The MacLeod Report, p. 13.
2. Ibid., p. 16: "The Committee agrees with the widely held opinion that approximately seventy-five per cent of the program of teacher education should be devoted to academic studies and approximately twenty-five per cent to professional preparation" — in other words, three years academic and one year professional.
3. Ibid., p. 24: "However, mere knowledge of a subject, while extremely important, is insufficient qualification for teaching."
4. Floyd Robinson et al., *Volunteer Helpers in Elementary Schools: A Survey of Current Practice in the Niagara Region and an Analysis of Instructional Roles* (Toronto: Ontario Institute for Studies in Education, 1971), p. 4.
5. *Religious Information and Moral Development: The Report of the Committee on Religious Education in the Public Schools of the Province of Ontario 1969,* J. Keiller Mackay, chairman (Toronto: Ontario Department of Education, 1969), p. 64.

A Diploma of Further Studies in Education

V. S. Ready

With the rapid changes taking place in education in our schools today, there is at least one idea for which there is almost unanimous support within the teaching profession: that teachers must engage in ongoing programs of continuing education if they are to be worthy of the name *professional*. This need for further study is intensified as the Ministry transfers to teachers increased responsibility for curriculum design and development. Indeed, there is considerable support for the argument that teachers should initially be certified only for a specific period of time and that they should show evidence of having engaged in further study before their certificates are renewed for another term.

At present, a variety of courses, workshops, seminars, and educational activities are available to teachers for their professional improvement. Many teachers have taken advantage of these offerings, and others continue to do so. The programs are provided by several agencies, including the teachers' federations, the universities, teacher training institutions, and the Ministry of Education. Some carry credits toward additional degrees or certificates, but most do not. There is a need for all these activities to be coordinated so that clear lines of professional growth can be planned and credited to a teacher's record.

With teaching now becoming largely a degree-based profession, there will be a growing impetus toward further education on the part of a larger segment of the teaching force. One way to meet this demand is to expand opportunities for graduate studies in education. Several universities are planning graduate programs in education, and an increasing number of teachers are looking toward master's and doctoral programs in this and other disciplines. It is not at all clear, however, that the Ontario government is prepared to fund graduate programs on a scale necessary to meet the anticipated demand.

The graduate route is not the only alternative in continuing education. Some teachers will want to devote their energies to more "practical," or applied, activities, rather than follow courses in educational theory leading to a degree. Others will prefer a more diverse package of activities than is possible in a structured degree program, or they may want to undertake a series of short workshop activities in lieu of longer courses.

One shortcoming of the present system is that there is no way in Ontario for teachers to gain recognizable credit for the various legitimate educational activities in which they participate outside formal programs of study. For this reason, many teachers are enrolling in graduate studies programs that lead to a tangible recognition of effort (a degree), when in fact other routes in continuing education would be more appropriate to their particular needs.

It is therefore proposed that we consider for Ontario a Diploma of Further Studies in Education, which would be recognized by the Ministry of Education, the teachers' federations, and boards and universities. These agencies would have strong reasons for supporting such a diploma, for all are interested in developing better qualified and more competent teachers. The diploma would provide a flexible instrument for measuring the various applied professional skills of teachers, in contrast to the formal graduate degree, which is awarded under stringent university criteria of academic theoretical rigor. In addition, programs for diploma credits would be less expensive to mount, prepare, and offer than graduate courses. The awarding of the diploma would best be administered by a provincial office, perhaps located within the Ontario Teachers' Federation or the Ministry. Its operation should be regulated by a provincial board made up of representatives of the federations, the Ministry, the faculties of education, and the trustees' councils. Any institution offering continuing education activities could apply to this board for recognition of its program as a credit toward the diploma. Credit could be based on the number of hours completed in each specific activity.

There are several ways in which these accumulating credits could be used.

1. A certain number of credit hours could fulfill the requirements for the renewal of a basic term certificate.
2. The diploma (and certain credit levels within it), once earned, could be recognized within the certification charts of the federations.
3. The diploma (and certain credit levels within it), once earned, could be recognized within salary structures in the province.
4. The diploma could be used as part of the admission requirements for graduate degrees and might carry some credits into the master's degree program.

This last use could be a distinct advantage in helping a candidate to prove professional competence to undertake graduate study. Universities generally have insisted upon evidence of scholarship as a first condition for undertaking a master's degree. Few would quarrel with this as a matter of principle, but the difficulty in the field of education is that the conditions under which many teachers took their first degree mitigated against their acquiring an impressive scholarly record. A large number acquired their degrees through extension courses and were thus required to piece together a degree program from whatever courses happened to be offered in a particular summer school. Often the courses were not the ones they would have preferred, often they were offered in a haphazard order, and often they were conducted by individuals who were not accredited university instructors. Thus, many teachers possess degrees that look "weak" by graduate school admission standards. Yet some of these teachers have proven in their professional careers to be most competent teachers and administrators. In such cases, it seems grossly unfair to deny these people the right to attempt graduate studies. The diploma with good standing might well provide the additional evidence needed to give these individuals an opportunity to enroll in a master's program.

In fact, some institutions have already begun granting diplomas in further education on the basis of the educational offerings they currently have available. But such isolated initiatives, however well intentioned, will only add to the existing fragmentation and incoherence in this area. Before this development proceeds further, we should give serious thought to creating a more universal diploma, accepted across the province, toward which many institutions could contribute. Such an action would give teachers a wide choice among the components of their diploma program. In our mobile society, portability of credit seems appropriate, particularly in the field of continuing education.

One of the activities that the regulatory board could consider for credit is the individual's work as an associate teacher in conjunction with a faculty of education. Teachers engaged in this essential part of teacher training provide a highly useful service to the profession; but in addition, almost without exception, they claim that the experience contributes to their personal and professional growth. The experience is even more stimulating when the associate teachers and other members of faculties develop close working relationships on an ongoing basis.

The costs involved in setting up a provincial coordinating office for a diploma should not inhibit serious consideration of this proposal. Data systems can go a long way toward simplifying the record-keeping for individual teachers. There may be ways in which such record-keeping could be tied in with the Ministry proposals for maintaining a teacher's record as part of the professional certificate. In any event, the advantages for growth within the teaching profession inherent in the rationalization of continuing education activities amply justify the initial difficulties or expense entailed in creating such a diploma.

Bridging the Gap: Improving Cooperation between Teacher Educators and Teachers

George S. Tomkins

My own interest in this topic arose out of my work on the COFFE Report (Commission on the Future of the Faculty of Education) at the University of British Columbia in 1968/69, and my involvement since mid-1971 in the work of the Canada Studies Foundation.[1] The COFFE Report represented an attempt to define new approaches to teacher education in terms of *integration* of the student teacher's pre-service experience, *specialization* (drawing largely on Macdonald's model of professionalism),[2] and *a gradual and sequential introduction to the teaching task* (drawing again on Macdonald and also on B. Othanel Smith),[3] the whole culminating in a sustained school experience, controlled by the faculty but shared with the field, and a further on-campus training period.

In retrospect, the weaknesses of the COFFE Report are evident enough. It was prepared during the first stage of serious ferment about teacher education in the United States and the United Kingdom and thus had value in drawing the attention of Canadians to developments in these countries, but it suffered the limitations of being a pioneering attempt. While I am not sure that its approach to specialization can be defended now, I am sure that it failed to anticipate the needs and possibilities of in-service teacher education and the concept of continuing education. Its efforts to face up to the crucial question of improving the relationship between faculty and field were welcome, but inadequate. The COFFE Report remained well within the tradition of Canadian teacher education in assuming that a pre-service program could turn out a finished product.

My involvement with the Canada Studies Foundation has given me fresh opportunities to think about teacher education. The Foundation's work is in a real sense a teacher education enterprise based on the radical notion that teachers can and should play a central role in curriculum development. My own work as director of the curriculum projects now operating in all ten provinces has given me first-hand acquaintance with representatives of departments of education, teachers' associations, universities, and school systems, and has introduced me to the grassroots problems of teacher education.

My observations regarding Canadian teachers, arising from discussions with hundreds of them in their schools and classrooms, have led me to several general conclusions regarding their current professional activities and interests. First of all, in spite of all the rhetoric about the changing role of the teacher, the teacher's instructional role remains paramount. Teachers are still teaching. Most continue to do so against the considerable odds familiar to all of us. What is encouraging is how many are trying to break out of traditional straitjackets and are responding to the new challenges facing them. Second, although we have plenty of creative or potentially creative teachers in Canada, at present they sadly lack the skills they require for decision making in their instructional role. This is an old and familiar problem; the wonder is that — again, given the constraints under which they operate — so many function as well as they do. Teachers generally lack skill in defining the goals and objectives of the instructional programs for which they are responsible, in contributing to the processes of curriculum development, and in evaluating themselves, their students, their programs, and their institutions.

These considerations lead me to the strongest conviction I have formed about both pre-service and in-service teacher education, namely, that *it should focus on curriculum development and associated skills*. I use the term *development* broadly here to include not only the building and planning of curriculum or its segments ("units"), but also the interpretation and modification of existing curricula. This conviction is further strengthened by the fact that the decentralization of programs and curricula that has occurred in nearly all provinces makes it essential that teachers undertake these responsibilities. Teachers have always filled a role as interpreters of curricula; now a more comprehensive and challenging task is being thrust upon them. Many use their new freedom creatively. Many more are lost because they lack the skills required for such a role.

If teachers are to become effective curriculum developers as well as interpreters and implementers, then curriculum development must become the focus for teacher education at both the pre-service and the in-service stages. As Tyler suggests, four fundamental questions must be asked and answered if there is to be an effective basis for curriculum development:

1. What educational purposes should the school seek to attain?
2. What educational experiences can be provided that are likely to attain these purposes?
3. How can these educational experiences be effectively organized?
4. How can we determine whether these purposes are being attained?[4]

In order to deal with these complex questions, teachers will have to develop a wide range of curriculum skills. They must learn to think more systematically about the goals and objectives of what they teach, to identify and modify the aims of curricula developed by others, and to recognize that objectives frequently emerge during, as well as before, the learning process, with unexpected outcomes. Certainly, teachers must have not only a scholarly content base, but a theoretical base in terms of the learning process. But beyond this, they need much more skill and practice in evaluating and selecting which procedures and content areas they wish to use. Experience elsewhere — with American summer institutes, for example — suggests that any approach to curriculum development that relies solely on upgrading teachers' subject knowledge is unlikely to be effective. In value-laden fields particularly (and Canadian studies is clearly one of these), where the consideration and discussion of controversial or unresolved issues is vital, teachers need to draw upon the insights of social psychologists, educational philosophers, and others, as well as of scholars in the subject disciplines of history, economics, and the like.

In a recent paper, Geraldine Channon describes the teacher as curriculum developer in terms that emphasize the "continual methods, resources and approaches which lead to increased learning," and the "critical examination of the value of what it is proposed should be learned."[5] Similarly, Michael Connelly sees the teacher in relation to curriculum development as an instructional decision maker — one who, by a process of rational deliberation, makes choices appropriate to his teaching conditions, choosing from the wide array of possibilities that any curriculum presents.[6] His "choice and deliberation project" at the Ontario Institute for Studies in Education involves practicing science teachers in one of the most promising in-service curriculum training programs anywhere in Canada. Analogous to it is the Vancouver Environmental Education Project directed by C. J. Anastasiou at the University of British Columbia.

Curriculum development as a focus for teacher education could operate across the whole spectrum, from the undergraduate pre-service through the graduate in-service and continuing levels. For the pre-service teacher, it is not hard to imagine the various roles that could be played, from teacher aide, through research assistant, to intern, all related to tasks of curriculum development focused on curriculum projects of varying scope, from units to full courses or programs. Such participation would provide a gradual and varied introduction to the teaching task. It would make "methods courses" (assuming that these continue) more relevant and realistic, and the same would apply to the school experience, which could assume many forms in addition to conventional practice teaching. Student teachers would no longer, it is hoped, be seen as intruders in classrooms; rather, they would be members of a curriculum development team, working with their supervising teachers, for whom the work might well be a part of in-service training. Thus, curriculum development could provide the needed link between pre-service and in-service teacher education. For faculty members, curriculum development could provide the necessary link between theory and practice, and between faculty and field.

Several factors indicate that teacher education can be improved significantly over the next few years. A new generation of leaders is appearing on the scene. In the last year or two, a dozen new deans of education have been appointed across the country. And a new generation of faculty has already appeared. During the past five years, a corps of bright, well-trained, articulate, and committed people have entered faculties. Overall, teacher educators seem to recognize and acknowledge the weaknesses of existing programs and are seriously interested in exploring alternative approaches.

Perhaps the most pressing priority is for the faculties of education to begin to see themselves as professional faculties rather than as miniature (or second-rate) arts faculties. This will require drastic changes in organization and emphasis, because most faculties are based on the university arts model. A much higher priority must be given to systematic planning and evaluation of the teacher education program if the faculties are to retain any credibility. A curriculum development focus in pre-service teacher education would mean a great reduction in discipline-centered courses in education. Most student teachers would be enrolled in a single major subject that would encompass most of their experience. This major would be curriculum development. Within the major, however, students might specialize, as now, in certain teaching subjects, in interdisciplinary studies, or in instructing certain categories of children. Some of the possibilities are outlined in chapters 2 and 3 of the COFFE Report.

If programs could be organized with curriculum development and the associated skills as a focus, a long step would have been taken toward the integration of pre-service programs. As an aspect of this, much better use could be made of foundations expertise. Although formal substantive foundations courses should come after the student has had a sustained exposure to practice (and might even be deferred to the in-service phase), the new breed of young foundations faculty can offer much to programs focused on curriculum development. This can best be done through short courses, workshop sessions, and similar offerings (for example, a sociologist could help students to perceive how social class factors operate as constraints in planning curriculum or a philosopher could give them training in concept definition).

Departmentalization, if not abandoned altogether, should be sharply reduced, and experiments instituted that enable faculty and students to work together in areas (not all of them necessarily permanent) in which the foci of endeavor can change as needed. Such areas might include communications education, values education, environmental education, urban education, cross-cultural education, and special education — to name but a few possibilities.

Above all, the faculties must abandon the idea that any pre-service program can prepare a finished product. We must, in short, abandon our faith in initial training and shift much of our focus to in-service training. The faculties must convey, through precept and practice, the realization that teaching is indeed a lifelong process of learning. The faculty, in association with the field, may then come to be perceived by teachers as, as Channon puts it, "a resource to which they may return throughout their careers for guidance, discussion and the examination and testing of ideas."[7] Narrow specialization should be avoided at the pre-service stage. This means that many options should be open to each teacher for changing or renewing specialties throughout his career. To this end, faculties will need to organize more flexible diploma and graduate degree programs.

It is at the in-service level that curriculum development as a focus is likely to be most fruitful. This concept comes at a most opportune time; in-service and continuing education are assuming growing importance and may soon overshadow the pre-service phase. Our present overdependence on initial training and the almost total abrogation of responsibility for the fate of the beginning teacher by all concerned, including the faculties of education, can no longer be tolerated. A plan similar to that proposed in the James Report in Great Britain, whereby the beginner has a reduced teaching load and ample opportunity for further training, has obvious implications for a curriculum development focus.[8] The experienced teacher, who has much to contribute to curriculum development, would continue his own education according to a flexible format ranging from the one-day workshop to paid sabbatical leave for full-time graduate study as a member of a curriculum development team.

A link would therefore be provided between graduate and undergraduate teacher education, since it can be assumed that the returning teacher could contribute to the latter, thus helping to refresh the training institution while himself being refreshed. His refreshment might well include training in a new specialty, for, while a degree of specialization can be assumed at the pre-service level, in-service education must be varied and flexible enough to permit the teacher to pursue new interests as well as to enhance old ones.

In the Canada Studies Foundation, we have begun to think of a leadership training plan in curriculum for a cadre of the ablest teachers we have identified in our work so far. This would involve providing training in curriculum leadership analogous to the training for administrative leadership that was initiated by the Kellogg program fifteen or twenty years ago. It is hoped that such a plan could be implemented at three or four centers in Canada — not necessarily at universities — on a cooperative basis involving provincial teachers' associations, departments of education, urban school systems, and faculties of education. A means could thus be provided for testing out ideas for various types of faculty–field relationships. From these could grow a series of model teacher education programs in faculties of education across Canada. Each of these programs might develop along distinctive lines, but they would all be based on careful planning and systematic evaluation. Greater efforts will need to be made to exchange information and to discuss openly and critically the problems and achievements of these programs. No longer can or should faculties of education remain isolated, defensive, parochial provincial institutions. The recently organized Canadian Society for the Study of Education may provide an appropriate forum for discussions and exchanges.

The possibilities of developing promising new directions are enormous. Of course, each teacher education institution should select only one or two new approaches and should try to explore fully their implications. Among the many possibilities, I would like to see the following initiated in this country:

1. The organization of a curriculum institute on a provincewide or regional basis to promote curriculum development as an essential part of undergraduate pre-service, in-service, continuing, and graduate teacher education programs.

2. The organization of two or three "training complexes" of the type Smith outlined in *Teachers for the Real World*.

3. The organization of a group of British-style teachers' centers in a medium-sized urban school system or in a small province or region.

4. The establishment by a faculty of education of a full-scale division

of field development, in-service, and continuing education, integrating functions now performed in various sections of most faculties — from standard student teaching to the offering of off-campus graduate courses. Such a division could service the full continuum of teacher education, from beginning pre-service to graduate programs in curriculum development. It would have to be organized and administered in cooperation with all concerned groups in the field.

5. The inception of a pilot cooperative in-service program bringing together the widest possible range of professionals and institutions concerned with childhood and youth (health-science personnel, teachers, social workers, librarians, and the like). This could be done under the aegis of a training center, such as a "complex" or a teachers' center. The focus of such a program could be, quite simply, children's learning.

6. The inception of a pilot program focusing on the first year of teaching, based on the proposals of the James Report in Great Britain, whereby the novice carries a 60 to 80 percent normal load and has time free for in-service training conducted cooperatively by the faculty of education and local school personnel. This is a variant of the "associateship" program recommended by the COFFE Report, and it could be organized in a great number of different ways. It would seem to be related to the concept of differentiated staffing (one of the lost opportunities of the 1960s). Model experiments in differentiated staffing could be conducted on a cooperative basis by faculties of education and school systems.

7. The exploitation by faculty and field personnel of the many opportunities for cooperative relationships presented by various other innovative or alternative education proposals — for example, a pilot "voucher plan," a "high school without walls" plan, a quasi-apprenticeship plan whereby high school students spend a large proportion (up to half) of their time gaining experience in a variety of community agencies, institutions, and business enterprises.[9]

There are two possible obstacles to these developments, obstacles that can be overcome but about which it is essential to be aware. The first is the attitude of teachers. Professionalism as a model, in the terms that Macdonald defined it in *The Discernible Teacher*, does not seem to have gained any ground in the past five years. The "personal service" model that Macdonald criticized remains dominant, but it is being increasingly challenged by the "trade union" model. If this "union" tendency takes a primarily defensive, protective direction — and, with the current political and economic pressures on the school system and on teachers, this is a distinct possibility — then it may be extremely difficult to obtain cooperation from the field in some of the innovative programs outlined above. Without that participation and cooperation, those programs are doomed to irrelevance.

The other side of the union model coin is that it seems to represent a new kind of teacher militancy, a determination by classroom teachers, in particular, to participate much more fully and independently in all phases of education policy and programs. This is indeed a hopeful sign and could, in fact, prove even more beneficial than the traditional "professional" model. Many teachers seem to want to rely much less on the educational hierarchy, on government direction, and on outside experts than they have in the past. Instead, they seem determined to develop their own knowledge, skills, and confidence, and to assume a new partnership status in education. This is a determination that faculties of education should respond to enthusiastically. If teacher educators deal with their colleagues in the field openly, candidly, and as full partners in a joint enterprise, then truly significant educational improvements and reforms can be made. Certainly, it has been the experience of the Canada Studies Foundation that Canadian teachers are equal to this challenge.

The other problem of which account must be taken is the traditions and nature of the university. In a number of ways, the university environment is hostile to the concerns of teacher education and tends to be inflexible in structure and organization. The directions discussed above require that new forms and approaches be sought. Fortunately, under the impact of declining enrollment, universities are becoming more receptive to continuing education. Above all, the universities, and particularly their teacher education faculties, must grasp and act on the fact that the improvement of teacher education — through a curriculum development focus or by any other means — can be achieved only by fully involving the classroom teachers in the field on a truly cooperative, collegial basis.

NOTES

1. *The Report of the Commission on the Future of the Faculty of Education*, G. S. Tomkins, chairman (Vancouver: University of British Columbia Press, 1969), referred to hereafter as the COFFE Report. The Canada Studies Foundation is an independent nonprofit foundation incorporated in February 1970. Since its inception, the CSF has addressed itself to the problems and failings in the field of Canadian studies, documented in Hodgetts's *What Culture? What Heritage?* It is currently supporting a number of curriculum development projects across the country in which classroom teachers play a central role. The Foundation's work is also notable in that each of its projects brings together teachers and other educators from different regional and/or linguistic groups in Canada.

2. John Macdonald, *The Discernible Teacher* (Ottawa: Canadian Teachers' Federation, 1970).

3. Smith et al., *Teachers for the Real World*.

4. Ralph W. Tyler, *Basic Principles of Curriculum and Instruction* (Chicago: University of Chicago Press, 1950), pp. 1–2.

5. Geraldine Channon, "Long Range Goals for the Development of Quality Teacher Education" (Ottawa: Canadian Teachers' Federation, 1973), p. 4.

6. F. Michael Connelly, "The Functions of Curriculum Development," *Interchange* 3, nos. 2–3 (1972): 161–77.

7. Channon, "Long Range Goals," p. 6.

8. *Teacher Education and Training: A Report by a Committee of Inquiry Appointed by the Secretary of State for Education and Science, under the Chairmanship of Lord James of Rusholme* (London: H.M.S.O., 1972).

9. See James S. Coleman's intriguing article, "How Do the Young Become Adults?," *Phi Delta Kappan* 54, no. 4 (December 1972): 226–30.

LIST OF CONTRIBUTORS

Robert Beardsley is a secondary school mathematics teacher and is at present Co-ordinator of Toronto's first alternative school program, SEED (Shared Experience, Exploration, and Discovery).

Brian S. Crittenden, formerly on the faculty of the Ontario Institute for Studies in Education, teaches philosophy and is a professor of education at La Trobe University, in Melbourne, Australia.

Jack H. Duthie teaches educational psychology and is a senior lecturer in the Department of Education, University of Stirling, Scotland.

Robert Gidney teaches history of education at Althouse College of Education, University of Western Ontario, London.

Eric S. Hillis, formerly on the staff of the Atlantic Institute of Education in Halifax, Nova Scotia, is completing doctoral studies at the Faculty of Education, University of Alberta, Edmonton.

Myer Horowitz is Dean of the Faculty of Education, University of Alberta, Edmonton.

Philip Linden teaches English at Althouse College of Education, University of Western Ontario, London.

Robert Logan teaches in the Department of Physics at the University of Toronto.

Donald Longwell is a member of the primary school specialist staff of the Toronto Teachers' College.

John McMurtry teaches in the Department of Philosophy at the University of Guelph.

Geoffrey Milburn is Chairman of the History Department at Althouse College of Education, University of Western Ontario, London.

Douglas Myers teaches history in the Department of History and Philosophy at the Ontario Institute for Studies in Education, Toronto.

V. S. Ready is Dean of the Faculty of Education at Queen's University, Kingston.

Fran Reid is a research officer in the Department of History and Philosophy at the Ontario Institute for Studies in Education in Toronto.

David Saul is Special Consultant to the Department of Education, in Hamilton, Bermuda.

Verner Smitheram is Chairman of the Department of Philosophy in the Faculty of Education at the University of Prince Edward Island, Charlottetown.

John A. Tickle is Superintendent of Schools for the Niagara South Board of Education, Welland.

George S. Tomkins is Director of Projects for the Canada Studies Foundation, on leave of absence from the Department of Social Studies, Faculty of Education, University of British Columbia, Vancouver.

Other OISE publications of concern in teacher education

Learning to Be: The World of Education Today and Tomorrow
International Commission on the Development of Education, Unesco (Chairman: Edgar Faure)
A search for solutions to the development of education in our changing world. This report offers a critical assessment of the educational situation in twenty-three countries and makes a serious attempt to discern new trends and identify "dead ends." The central concern is to find concrete ways in which education can be made relevant to society's needs, accessible to all, and part of a lifelong process.   313 pages, 1973.

Key Issues in Higher Education
Edward B. Harvey and Jos L. Lennards
Insights into the problems of the "multiversity." In this study, the authors survey related research, examine opinions about the goals of the university, and propose organizational changes in our system of higher education that will enable it to meet the multiple demands made on the modern university. Consideration is given to such questions as the benefits a university offers, its effectiveness as an agent of attitude change, and equality of educational opportunity.   128 pages, 1973.

Teacher Education in Prince Edward Island
Willard Brehaut
An attempt to pinpoint the types of teacher education programs needed in P.E.I. The author gives a brief account of the development of teacher education in the province and offers proposals for pre-service and in-service programs.   59 pages, 1972.

Psychology in Teacher Preparation
John Herbert and David P. Ausubel, Editors
Views on the relationship of psychological theory to classroom practice. The contributors to this collection of papers describe existing courses in educational psychology being offered to teachers in Canada and abroad, examine some of the fundamental problems in training teachers in educational psychology, and propose ways of bridging the distance between the behavioral sciences and education. 128 pages, 1969.

THE IN-BASKET SIMULATION SERIES
Donald F. Musella and H. Donald Joyce
A series of booklets designed to simulate the problems encountered by administrators at various levels of the education system. The reader is placed in a hypothetical situation that challenges his judgment on how best to deal with problems of the sort the administrator may encounter in a normal day. Titles in the series are:

The Elementary School Principal   40 pages, 1972.

The Elementary School Consultant   1974.

The Intermediate School Principal   39 pages, 1973.

The Secondary School Principal   40 pages, 1973.

The Secondary School Division Chairman   37 pages, 1974.

The Area Superintendent   50 pages, 1973.

The Director of Education   63 pages, 1973.

The School Board Trustee   43 pages, 1973.

Also available is an instructional handbook, *Conducting In-Basket Simulation: A Handbook for Workshop Leaders*, which suggests how these materials can be used.   82 pages, 1973.

The catalogue listing these and other OISE publications may be obtained from Publications Sales, The Ontario Institute for Studies in Education, 252 Bloor Street West, Toronto, Ontario M5S 1V6.